Photography
Eiji Kōri

Translation
Juliet Winters Carpenter

KODANSHA INTERNATIONAL LTD.
Tokyo, New York, and San Francisco

A FEAST FOR THE EYES

The Japanese Art of Food Arrangement

Yoshio Tsuchiya

Food Arrangement
Masaru Yamamoto

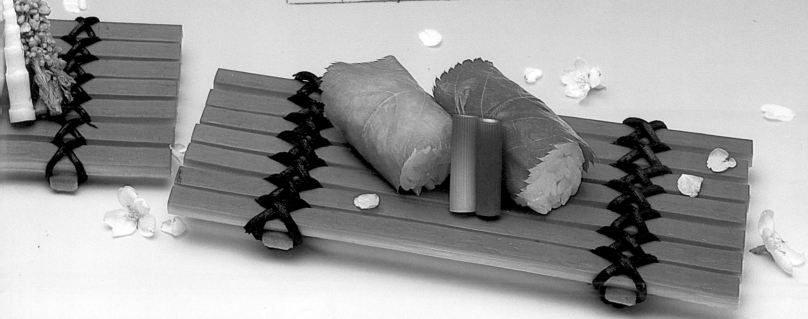

Publication of this book was assisted by a grant from the Japan Foundation.

Distributed in the United States by Kodansha International/USA Ltd., through
Harper & Row, Publishers, Inc., 10 East 53rd Street, New York, New York
10022. Published by Kodansha International Ltd., 12-21, Otowa 2-chome,
Bunkyo-ku, Tokyo 112 and Kodansha International/USA Ltd., with offices
at 10 East 53rd Street, New York, New York 10022 and the Hearst Building,
5 Third Street, Suite No. 430, San Francisco, California 94103.

   LCC 84-48699
   ISBN 0-87011-718-1
   ISBN 4-7700-1218-7 (in Japan)
First edition, 1985

Library of Congress Cataloging-in-Publication Data

Tsuchiya, Yoshio, 1938–
     A feast for the eyes.

     Includes index.
     1. Food presentation. 2. Table setting and
decoration—Japan. 3. Tableware—Japan. 4. Cookery,
Japanese. I. Title.
TX652.T795 1985   641.5952   84-48699
ISBN 0-87011-718-1 (U.S.)

CONTENTS

INTRODUCTION

The art of arranging food on serving dishes is expressed in Japanese by the verb *yosou*, which also means "to dress up" or "ornament." This overlap of meanings is fitting, since the arrangement of Japanese dishes is traditionally an aesthetic and creative act. The result is an unsurpassed harmony between food and vessel— a harmony that captures the character of Japanese cuisine.

Why have the Japanese paid such attention to food arrangement and serving vessels? To answer this question, one must examine Japanese eating habits. Traditionally, the Japanese people took their meals seated directly on tatami floor matting, with a small tray-table for each person—a conspicuous difference from Europe or China, where diners sit in chairs around a common dining table. Also, unlike countries where everyone serves himself or herself from a large dish, in Japan individual servings are laid out beforehand on each tray-table and carried in to the diners.

Luis Frois (1532–97), a Portuguese priest who lived in Japan in the latter half of the sixteenth century, observed, "We [Europeans] keep the table out before the food is ready to serve, while they [Japanese] bring the table in from the kitchen already set with food."

This striking difference—on the one hand, people sitting together around one table, on the other people seated in a row, each facing an individually set tray-table—goes far to explain the development of the Japanese art of food arrangement. Dishes laid out on a tray or tabletop some thirty centimeters square can be taken in at a single glance, the diner relishing the exquisite harmony of color, shape, and texture before him as if surveying foothills from a mountain peak. This visual pleasure is an indispensable prelude and accompaniment to the savory pleasures that follow.

The more colorful and varied the "scenery," the greater the diner's pleasure. An Edo period cookbook called *Kasen no kumi-ito* (1748) offers the following advice: "Take special care with color combinations, seasoning, and arrangement. First, omit none of the five colors: green, yellow, red, white, and black. Second, take all of the five flavors fully into account. Third, if a dish of *namasu* [raw fish and vegetables in vinegar], for example, is to be made in the shape of a landscape, you must contrive to see that all else conforms to the same pattern as well.''

The ''five colors'' and ''five flavors'' mentioned here show the influence of ancient Chinese beliefs based on the principles of *yin* and *yang*, and the five natural elements: fire, wood, earth, metal, and water.

This philosophy gave rise to the bright colors and striking contrasts in appearance and flavor that are hallmarks of fine Japanese cuisine.

The five flavors are hot, tart, bitter, sweet, and salty; the five culinary arts, to serve raw, boil, grill, steam, and fry.

According to this philosophy, everything in the universe arises from the opposing, balancing principles of *yin* and *yang*; of the five elements, wood and fire belong to *yang* and metal and water to *yin*, with earth in the center. The ebb and flow of *yin* and *yang* were said to account for all change and upheaval in nature and human affairs.

Another feature that helps to account for the visual beauty of Japanese cooking is the prevailing idea that dishes ought to give a strong sense of the season. In Japan the seasons are sharply divided and each has its own bounty of foods from the sea, the mountains, and the fields. Dishes using fresh foods in season must be matched perfectly with vessels to form a beautiful, harmonious whole. As a result, the most valued tableware is that which conveys an appropriate sense of the time of year. For example, in spring when green bamboo is in season, it is used as tableware either cut horizontally or split crosswise to show off the nodes.

This sensitivity to the seasons has been most cultivated in the tea ceremony. In *kaiseki ryōri*, the select foods served on individual trays as part of the tea ceremony, special emphasis is laid on the ''three *ki*'': *kisetsu* (season), *ki* (vessel), and *kikai* (occasion). The point is not to use unusual materials or display costly tableware. Rather, the most is made of each unique occasion, heightening hospitality by preparing and serving fresh foods in season to bring out the innate flavor, aroma, and color of the ingredients. Timing is essential: one must be alert to the guests' state of mind, offering the meal at the proper juncture.

A final distinguishing feature of Japanese cuisine is the beauty of the utensils themselves. Representative of Japanese table utensils are bowls and other vessels made of unfinished wood, designed to bring out the natural grain, and lacquer ware of rich vermilion and black. Japanese people love the warmth of wood; they cherish its pleasant feel against the skin and its comfortable weight in the hands. Metal bowls and other vessels, such as those used in Korea, were introduced to Japan no later than the eighth century and were among the dishes used by the Heian period (794–1185) courtiers. Gradually, however, metal vessels went out of use. The hardness and chill of metal is not congenial to the traditional Japanese way of eating with bowl in one hand and chopsticks in the other.

More recently, Japan has produced pottery of such versatility and beauty that demand for it has spread overseas. Today the Japanese table is set with a variety of utensils, each with its own distinctive charm: the elegance of lacquer mixes easily with stoneware and porcelain, no one material predominant.

When multicolored foods are arranged on serving dishes, great attention is given to the matter of spacing—where and how to leave empty areas to best emphasize the beauty of the dish. This is based on the concept of *ma*: space as a dynamic entity, and integral and vital component of any composition. Fundamentally, the same aesthetic principle is involved in a serving of Japanese sweets, as well as in the celebrated stone garden at Ryōan-ji, in the Katsura Detached Palace, and in a traditional tea room.

The German architect Bruno Taut (1880–1938), who celebrated the architectural sublimity of the Katsura Detached Palace, came to Japan in the year 1933. Following is his account of a meal served him in a Japanese home:

> Various dishes were laid on the table, each in its own receptacle. Broth was in a lacquer bowl, and for fish there was a plate of irregular shape, decorated with a glaze of a very subdued color that blended well with that of the bowl. Also there were a plate of yet another shape, heaped with red and white slices of raw fish; a small dish containing soy sauce to dip the slices in; a dish containing a salad-style serving of vegetables; a small bowl of pickles, to be eaten with rice; a covered bowl of rice and a little wine cup, along with a little *saké* bottle on a stand in the center of the table. . . .
>
> My wife in particular was wonderstruck at the beauty of the repast spread out before us. It would appear that the appetite of the Japanese is aroused principally through appeal to his optic nerves. The table was a picture. Mr. Mamada explained that the outstanding feature of Japanese cuisine lies not in the quality of the cooking itself, but rather in its elegant, visual means of presentation. Thus fish, vegetables and all are served in handsome containers, to achieve an effect that is highly aesthetic—indeed pictorial. In front of the

13

meal lay a pair of chopsticks, their ends resting on a tiny porcelain holder; the parallel lines formed by those two chopsticks, balanced against the layout of the entire meal, was particularly effective.

A common reaction of foreign visitors to Japan upon first experiencing a true Japanese meal is to liken the food and its arrangement to a still-life painting.

> The range and delicacy of Japanese sensibility . . . are displayed on the inner table in colors suggestive of Impressionist paintings: slices of raw fish in hues from bluish pearl to pink; gray shadows; ocher sea-urchin eggs. The red of ginger and vivid green of vegetables are complemented by the deep brown of mushrooms, and by bits of white rice wrapped in black seaweed, as if outlined in India ink. Tomatoes, cucumbers, onions and other vegetables are peeled and carved into intricate shapes.
> Enormous time, imagination and care go into the preparation of each element in the tableau, including eating utensils. Wooden chopsticks, which transform the fingers into a kind of antennae, are well suited for savoring small amounts of food; our own spoon and fork are suited rather for transporting large amounts of food to the mouth.
> ("First Impressions of Japan"—Rudolph Arnheim)

This book seeks to deepen an understanding of this combination of beauty and utility in Japanese serving vessels by tracing their development through the centuries.

I

SEASONAL FOOD ARRANGEMENTS

Spring

Summer

II

THE ART
OF
FOOD
ARRANGEMENT

Masaru Yamamoto

Sketches by
Shūki Matsuzaki

JAPANESE FOOD:
A FEAST FOR THE EYES

Japanese cooking, it is often said, is designed to be eaten with the eyes. It makes the most of the natural flavor of each ingredient and at the same time delights the eye with careful attention to vessels and the arrangement of food therein.

I believe that the appeal of fine cooking is never limited to the palate. All the senses are involved—sight, smell, and hearing too—in a total appreciation of the harmony of beauty and flavor.

As a chef of *kaiseki* cuisine, responsible every year for the training of new chefs, I have learned from experience that simply knowing how a dish is prepared is not enough. No less important is knowing how to make dining a pleasurable experience overall. Scrupulous attention must be paid to food arrangement, wares, service, cleanliness, and similar matters, all of which have bearing on the savoriness of a meal—and all of which contribute importantly to the special appeal of Japanese cuisine. A restaurant that understands this holistic approach to cooking is one whose clientele will be thoroughly satisfied. I make the creation of such satisfaction my constant goal.

The wares pictured here in the Seasonal Food Arrangements section typify the best in traditional Japanese utensils from the Muromachi, Momoyama, Edo, Meiji, and Shōwa periods. When food is arranged in them (when they are seen, in other words, as they were meant to be seen), they come alive in an amazing transfiguration. One can only marvel at the extraordinary care the Japanese people have expended over the centuries on eating utensils.

The Pleasure of Unmatched Dishes
In China and the West it is customary to serve meals in a set of matched dishes that vary only in size and shape. Tableware materials, moreover, are generally limited to metal, china, and glass.

But in Japan the *mukōzuke* dish for fresh raw fish, the bowl for clear or thick soup, the plate for grilled or deep-fried food—the receptacle for each separate item on the menu is unique, differing from the rest in shape, design, color, and, sometimes, material. The types and the combinations of receptacles used in a meal are important foci of the diner's appreciation. Dishes must be chosen to harmonize with and set off the foods served; indeed the choice of tableware alone can make the difference between a memorable meal and a mediocre one.

Once, the story goes, a Chinese woman lacking this understanding stayed with a Japanese family. At every meal the dishes set before her were, of course, unmatched, according to Japanese custom; the poor woman was taken aback at this shabby (from her point of view) treatment, and suffered for a long time from the dismal impression that she was being accorded a subtle form of discrimination.

Perhaps no other country uses such a variety of tableware as Japan. Besides the diversity of form related to function, there is a great variety of material, including lacquer, ceramics, bamboo, and plain wood. And there are innumerable kinds of ceramics, ranging from the soft warmth of Raku, Shino, and Kiseto wares to the earthy naturalness of Iga, Shigaraki, and Bizen wares, or the pristine elegance of Ninsei, Kakiemon, and enameled Nabeshima. Yet each style is uniquely Japanese.

To me, next to Chinese or Korean pottery, that of Japan always seems milder and more personal. Some might even say it is too informal. In any case, in *kaiseki* cuisine, a piece of some exquisite Chinese ware with an appeal to the intellect—detailed blue-and-white porcelain, for example—is often used for a tempering effect.

35

Among Japanese table implements are many considered appropriate to a particular season because of material, pattern, color, and shape. *Mukōzuke* dishes, in particular, come in a great variety of shapes: the clamshell shape goes with spring, the lily with early summer. Vessels in the shape of a split pod evoke an image of late summer.

The existence of such a tremendous range of vessels—deep, shallow, and of almost every conceivable shape—probably owes much to the practice of eating not with knife and fork, but with chopsticks.

Fig. 1. Lily-shaped dish

Vessels and Food Arrangement

Among the serving vessels that I used for this occasion are several by the Edo master Ogata Kenzan. Of these, the peony-shaped *mukōzuke* dishes are particularly beautiful, with a sense of lofty dignity and bold strength. I pondered long as to what sort of food Kenzan might have meant for them to hold. Finally I chose some ingredients for their color and arranged them in as natural a style as possible. When all was done, it was as if the dishes were warmly embracing the food. The uneven, slightly raised edges, like those on a serrated leaf, form an empty space of great aesthetic appeal.

Rosanjin Kitaōji, a brilliant modern potter, is known for highly individualistic creations that go far beyond mere imitations of the past. A great epicure and cook as well, he was dissatisfied with the dishes available commercially and set out in his forties to become a potter and make his own. He once said, "The quality of food truly goes hand in hand with that of the dishes it is served in. It will not do for either one to be inferior to the other."

Not only are Rosanjin's dishes extremely easy to arrange any kind of food in, but they also enhance the appearance of the food. In addition, they are made with a careful eye to function: a square dish of seemingly artless design is actually contrived so that juices gather in the center; the bottom, moreover, is made so it does not scratch the tray it rests on. Even the rim is made for convenience in lifting. The outward appearance is one of solidity and weight, but held in the hands it is surprisingly light. Rosanjin's experience as a skilled cook undoubtedly contributed greatly to his achievements as a potter.

Rosanjin himself could arrange food beautifully, it is said. Simply, "Design a pattern or image with food," he advised, "just as you would with flowers [*ikebana*] or paints."

As this quotation suggests, the presentation of

Japanese food was traditionally impressionistic, with no firm rules. The only guidelines were to be absolutely natural; to use ingredients in season; to balance foods and vessels so that neither dominated the other; and to execute the arrangements swiftly, making them easy to eat and to dismantle with chopsticks. The way food is arranged in a dish can bring the dish to life or as easily kill it. Success requires both a love of food and an eye for beauty.

Certain pitfalls should be noted. Moving and reshaping the food once it is in place, for example, will only soil the dish. Also taboo is the sort of arrangement that collapses when a single piece is removed. Elaborate ways of cutting up an item of food or forcing it into a desired shape tend to create an impression of uncleanliness; generally it is better to alter the natural shape as little as possible. Inedible garnishes such as leaves and flowers should be avoided.

Food is the most basic requisite of life. Since we must all eat three times a day, every day, we might as well try to relish each meal. And preparing food that is at once tasty, easy to eat, and attractive has other less obvious benefits: it can hone our sensitivity, deepen our consideration of others, enrich our social contacts, bring zest to life.

I hope that people will experiment freely with Japanese techniques of arranging food and using vessels, incorporating them as they please in their accustomed routines. The Japanese art of food arrangement is neither precious nor inscrutable, but a way of greatly multiplying one's pleasure in the simple, creative, and universal act of preparing food.

PRINCIPLES AND STYLES OF JAPANESE FOOD ARRANGEMENT

The Beauty of Empty Space

The art of Japanese food arrangement is characterized by certain broad concepts, perhaps foremost among which is the concept that empty space has a beauty of its own. Indeed, the importance of "empty" space in the presentation of Japanese cuisine can scarcely be exaggerated. Receptacles are never filled to the brim, but are left with a certain margin of emptiness—emptiness of an aesthetic significance comparable to that in Zen ink painting. The balances between vessel and space, space and food, are crucial.

The balance varies according to the season, the design of the wares, and the type of food, as well as considerations like the place and even the age of the guests: a set amount of food may be too much for an elderly person, too little for a healthy young person. In summer a loose sort of arrangement seems oppressively warm, so the proportion of food is decreased slightly for a tighter, more disciplined appearance.

The amount of space considered appropriate also varies in different regions of the country. In the far north, for example, servings are generally larger than elsewhere (perhaps in part because of the harsh climate) and the margin of space is that much less. Kyoto, for centuries the imperial capital and the center of culture—including the tea ceremony—saw the preparation and serving of food develop into a highly refined art; the smallness of portions in Kyoto is not from stinginess or penury, therefore, but from a desire to stimulate eye and palate alike. At first sight, the impression may be one of oversimplicity; but ingredients are rigorously checked, and seasoning is deliberately light to keep from masking natural flavors. Infinite subtle pains are expended to make foods easier to eat: fish is always boned completely, and hard foods like pickled radish (*takuan*) are made edible for those with poor teeth by scoring them finely on the back with a knife, a technique called *kakushi bōchō* (''hidden knifework''). Such cuisine, at once simple and refined, is, I believe, representative of the finest in Japanese cooking.

The Beauty of Contrast

Suppose that round bowls and a round *mukōzuke* dish were placed together on a square *oshiki* tray: the effect would be stiff and uninteresting. Then what if a square *mukōzuke* dish was used? There would be contrast with the bowls, but the square of the *mukōzuke* would be repeated in that of the tray. For variety the square *mukōzuke* dish is turned slightly to form a diamond shape, creating a tasteful distribution of space. The use of contrasting shapes—round and square, long and short, large and small—causes each shape to stand out all the more. The same technique of contrast underlies the arrangement of food. Round foods go best in square containers, square foods in round.

Fig. 2. Round vessels on a round *oshiki* tray or a round *mukōzuke* dish used with round bowls—both arrangements lack interest. Varying shapes and angles make an arrangement more appealing.

Fig. 3. Square-shaped food is generally better in round vessels; round food in square vessels.

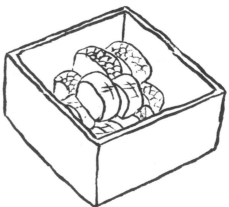

Shin, gyō, sō

The terms *shin*, *gyō*, and *sō* refer to three styles of calligraphy. *Shin* (''plain, true'') is the clear, basic style; *gyō* (''running'') a more cursive style; and *sō* (''grass''), a still more cursive form.

The same schema applies to food arrangement. A *shin*-style arrangement is one of precise order and dignity; in the *gyō*-style, foods are arranged in a slightly more relaxed manner, while the *sō* style is extremely casual—though still artistic—and hence unsuitable for an entire meal.

When a number of foods are arranged in a single container, a mixture of *shin*, *gyō*, and *sō* styles is best.

shin (formal)

gyō (running)

sō (''grass'')

Fig. 4. The three major styles of calligraphy. The Chinese character is ''vessel'' (*utsuwa*).

Preference for Odd Numbers

Sashimi is always presented in groups of three, five, or seven slices. The Japanese have an overwhelming predilection for odd numbers, based on the ancient Chinese philosophy of *yin-yang* and the five elements. According to this philosophy, even numbers are *yin* (dark, negative), and odd ones are *yang* (light, positive). This belief is reflected in Japanese cooking to this day.

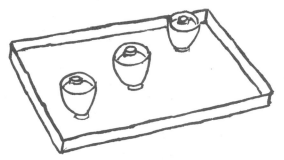

Fig. 5. Avoid arranging bowls symmetrically along the axis of a rectangular tray.

Yin and *yang* also contain the respective meanings of mournfulness and joyousness; to arrange foods in odd numbers is considered auspicious.

Because of the Western preference for even numbers, Western food tends to be flat and symmetrical in appearance. Such arrangements could be said to possess the beauty of regularity. The arrangement of Japanese food, in contrast, is asymmetrical and fluid, yet filled with a sense of quiet stability.

Color Harmony and Contrast

Color coordination will generally take care of itself if seasonal foods are used. When I realized this, I became much less concerned about technicalities of color combination. Spring foods used together will naturally produce fresh, springlike colors, while autumnal foods provide just the right set of colors for that time of year. For example, *matsutake*, a fall mushroom, does not go well with new green leaves, but can be paired beautifully with yellow *yuzu* citron.

The use of leaves as garnish is best kept to a minimum. Lately there is a tendency to serve food garnished with flowers—but if the room already contains an arrangement of cherry blossoms, to have cherry blossoms garnishing one's food as well can only detract from the arrangement. In general, I think it wise to avoid dressing food up with inedible garnishes; the food can and should speak for itself.

Styles of Japanese Food Arrangement

Cedar-Tree Style (*Sugimori*)

Sugimori is so called because food is piled up in a conal shape suggestive of cedar (*sugi*) trees. The empty space on all sides gives this arrangement an air of clean refinement. It is used often for *mukōzuke*, using thin slices of white-fleshed fish such as sea bream and sea bass. It is not suited for softer, red-fleshed fish.

Fillet the fish in the *sanmai-oroshi* technique (described on page 42) and remove skin and bones. Divide each fillet into top and bottom, and set lengthwise on the board with tail to the right. For sea bream and other meaty fish, first divide lengthwise into segments about 10 centimeters long; then, holding the blade flat, slice from right to left to adjust the thickness. Finally, cut each segment in narrow strips 4–5 millimeters across.

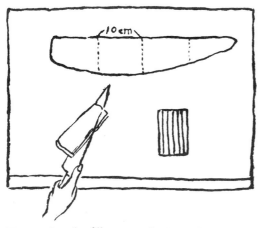

Fig. 6. Cut the fillet crosswise into 10-cm pieces, then cut any thick sections into thin, even slices. Cut the slices into narrow strips (4–5 mm).

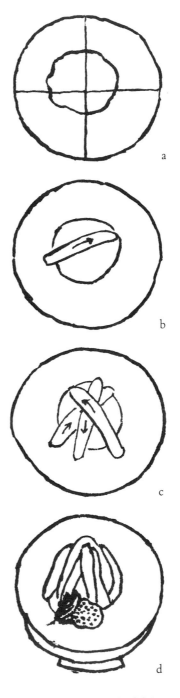

a

b

c

d

Fig. 7. a) Lay a small mound of fish just a bit to the rear of the vessel's center.
b, c) On this mound, arrange sashimi strips at different angles to form a stable cone form.
d) Arrange *wasabi* and garnish in front.

To arrange, lay a small mound of sashimi just a bit rear of center, then continue piling up the strips of fish in overlapping fashion to make a cone. The reason for positioning the food slightly off center, to the rear of the dish, has to do with the angle of view. Since the guest looks down diagonally from above, food placed slightly back will appear centered. If placed in the exact center, it seems too far forward, with a disproportionately large space behind.

The height of the cone varies according to the dish it is in. In shallow dishes it should rise slightly above the edge like a mountain peak jutting above clouds, while in a deeper dish the top of the cone should come just under the edge, to suggest cedar trees reaching up from a valley.

Fig. 8. Cedar tree

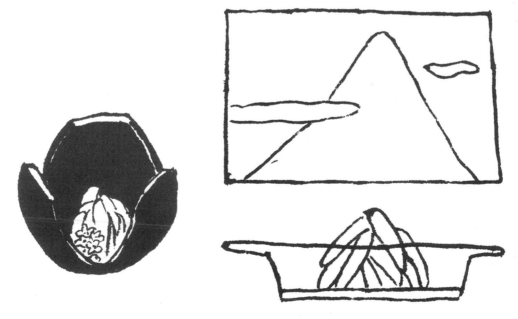

Fig. 9. When arranging food in a shallow dish, the arrangement should rise above the rim like a mountain above the clouds.

In a deep bowl, the food should come to just below the edge to suggest cedars reaching from a valley.

Flat Style (*Hiramori*)

This is a low, flat, horizontal arrangement ideal for a flat dish. Used widely for *sashimi*, it requires considerable cutting skill, but has the virtues of simplicity and manageability. With the *sashimi* arranged in a row, slightly forward on the left, and ground *wasabi* horseradish in the right front, guests find it easy to help themselves. Another advantage is the speed with which food can be arranged and served. (It is not considered suitable for *kaiseki*, however, for two reasons: it is a showy arrangement, and it frequently requires greater skill than the host—who presumably prepares the entire meal by hand—can command).

First the fish is filleted according to the "three-part slicing" technique (*sanmai oroshi*): two fillets are cut, one from each side of the fish, and the skeleton is left with some meat on it. Then each fillet is separated into top (center to spine) and bottom (center to belly) and laid skin-side up, lengthwise, with the thick side away from you. Ordinarily the skin is removed from the right end with the blade inclined a bit to the left. The knife should be drawn in a sweeping motion at an angle of about 15°. Start slicing at the right of the fish, pushing each slice a few inches to the right and laying it on its right side to form a neat row of "dominoes." The standard size for a slice is 5–8 millimeters.

Slices are transferred to plate or dish by scooping them up from the board five or seven at a time on the flat of the knife and setting them down on a slight diagonal, somewhat forward on the left and back on the right.

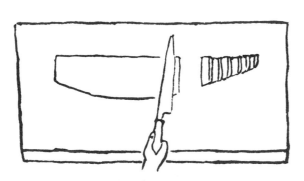

Fig. 10. Slicing sashimi

Fig. 11. Flat style

Bowl Style (*Wanmori*)

Wanmori is unique to *kaiseki*. The centerpiece of the *kaiseki* meal, it consists of abundant ingredients served in a clear soup, using a lacquer bowl larger than that for *miso* soup. A proper balance must be kept between the size of the bowl and the number of ingredients, so it is essential to begin by checking the size of the bowl.

First the ingredients are placed in the bowl a little to the rear of center. Then seasonal vegetables and greens are added for color. Greens such as chrysanthemum leaves should be placed straight across or tilted slightly up to the right (like the Chinese character for "one" —). (Whole cooked fish should be arranged on a plate the same way, with the head to the left, and tail slightly farther from the diner.)

One obvious practical advantage of lidded containers is that hot foods stay hotter in them. Beyond that, however, they allow guests to enjoy the pleasure of anticipation, building up in suspense to a small burst of surprise and admiration when the lid is at last removed. Care must be taken to keep the arrangement intact while carrying the bowl to the guest, to avoid spoiling this moment of discovery.

Besides this appeal to the imagination and the eye (not to mention the taste buds), lidded bowls offer another unexpected gratification—an olfactory one. Aromatic *yuzu* citron zest, cut in circles, trapezoids, and other shapes, is a frequent addition to *wanmori*. Known as *suikuchi*, it fills the air with a wonderful fragrance the instant the lid is removed.

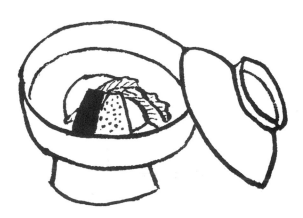

Fig. 12. Bowl style

Fig. 13. The Chinese character for "one" serves as a model for correctly arranged fish: the head at left is always slightly closer to the viewer than the tail at right.

Rice-Bale Style (*Tawaramori*)

Foods of a distinct shape (round, square, cylindrical, etc.) are piled like rice bales in a pyramid, with three on the bottom, two in the middle, and one on top as shown. Since items are of uniform size and shape, this arrangement is more geometric and precise than the "piled-up style." Put another way, the latter is *gyō* ("running, cursive"), and this is *shin* ("plain, basic").

Fig. 14. Stack of rice bales

Fig. 15. Rice-bale style

Piled-up Style (*Kasanemori*)

Pieces of boned fish, raw or grilled, are stacked one on another in an extremely casual and natural way, well suited to items of varying shape. The arrangement should also be neat and tight, with special care to ensure that the removal of one piece will not cause the entire pile to collapse. This style is good for grilled foods, since it retains heat well.

Fig. 16. Piled-up style

Jumbled Style (*Mazemori*)

This is a common way of arranging vegetables, used with combinations of differing shape and color (*takiawase*), vinegared vegetables (*sunomono*), vegetables dressed with sauce (*aemono*), and greens boiled then flavored with soy sauce (*hitashimono*).

Despite its name, the arrangement does not consist simply of heaping foods any old way. Rather, ingredients are arranged nicely in a small mound, with proper consideration for balance with the surrounding space. As with the cedar-tree style (of which it is a less precise form), the size of the arrangement is determined by the depth of the dish: in a shallow dish the mound should rise above the rim, while in a deeper one it should rise to about two-thirds the height of the dish.

After being heaped all at once in the dish, the ingredients are swiftly adjusted with chopsticks for a balanced distribution of color and shape.

Fig. 17. Jumbled style

Fig. 18. Two-ingredient nestled style

Nestled Style (*Yosemori*)

Two or three different ingredients are arranged side by side, nestled together in one dish. Usually fish or meat is the "main" ingredient, in combination with a lighter-flavored, secondary vegetable dish. The proportions of main and secondary ingredients are roughly equal, or that of the main ingredient may be slightly larger.

The main ingredient is placed in the front of the dish, the secondary one in the rear; they may be arranged in a straight line or one slanting diagonally right or left. In any case, the center of the arrangement is slightly back of the center of the dish.

First, the secondary ingredient is piled in the rear of the bowl, then the main ingredient is piled ("nestled") adjacent to it; so that the two will not appear randomly placed, it is important they they be arranged close together, facing center. Finally, in the center of the arrangement, an aromatic garnish is added—often a young sprig of *sansho* leaves in spring, green citron in summer, and yellow citron in fall and winter.

When three ingredients are used, the extra one is called a "supplement." Small in quantity, the supplement is used as a color highlight. First, the main ingredient is placed in the dish slightly rear of center. Then the secondary ingredient is added, taking care to leave space for the supplement. All three must closely touch, face the center, and be arranged for easy handling with chopsticks. Finally, if desired, a garnish is added on top, in the center of the arrangement.

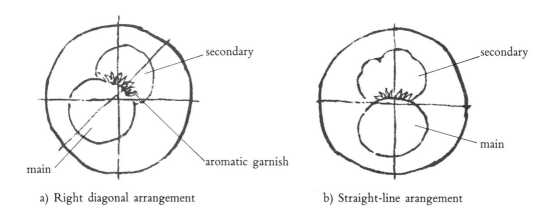

a) Right diagonal arrangement

b) Straight-line arangement

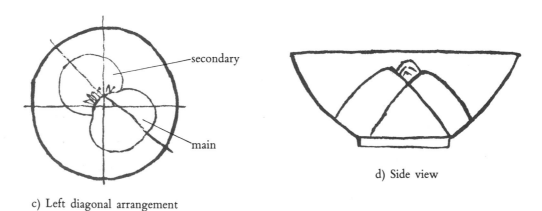

c) Left diagonal arrangement

d) Side view

Fig. 19. Two-ingredient nestled style

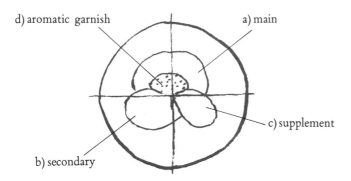

d) aromatic garnish

a) main

c) supplement

b) secondary

Fig. 20. Three-ingredient nestled style

Scattered Style (*Chirashimori*)

This style of food arrangement is used in *kaiseki* cooking with *hassun* trays—trays of plain cedar (usually) measuring just eight *sun* (1 *sun* = 3.3 cm) square. The wooden trays, *hassun*, which are immersed in water before using to protect them from stains, are brought out still gleaming wet and placed with the seam on the rim away from the guest. They hold "something from the land and something from the sea," or a harmonious combination of seafood (or poultry) and vegetables, arranged separately. The food is served as a slight, tasteful accompaniment to the exchange of saké cups between guest and host.

When more than two ingredients are used, repetitions of shape, color, and flavor must be avoided; the trick is to combine foods that form a distinctively contrasting yet harmonious ensemble. The contrast must not be too great, as between sweet foods and hot, spicy ones, for then the harmony is lost. Using two ingredients, salmon might be paired with long strips of

Fig. 21. Scattered style in *hassun* tray

mountain yam (*nagaimo*) for contrast of shape as well as color (reddish pink versus white) and taste (slightly pungent versus light). Another piquant combination is dried mullet roe and radish.

Some insist that the seafood be placed forward, the vegetables behind, to suggest a seascape with land on the horizon. Others insist that the seafood with its stronger odor should be on the far side, and the vegetables in front. I have no absolute preference either way. Yet spacing is indeed of utmost importance. The foods should be far enough apart to keep their flavors and aromas distinct.

If the surface of the tray is divided into thirds, both crosswise and lengthwise, the imaginary points of con-

tact in the upper right and lower left form the basis of the arrangement. (Food is placed not exactly on those points, but slightly off them, in the direction of their respective corners.) This ensures that both foods will be equally accessible; if lower right and upper left were used, most people would be forced to commit a breach of etiquette by reaching with chopsticks over the food in front of them to that behind.

The two items of food should not be arranged in the same style. Here again, variety is called into play; the sketch shows rice-bale style and piled-up style. The *shin-gyō-sō* pattern of precise adherence to a form, more relaxed adherence, and minimal adherence, may also be manipulated in interesting ways.

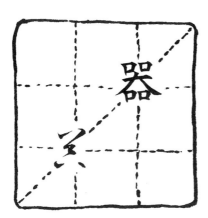

Fig. 22. The best position is usually just off the intersecting lines shone. Vary the arrangement styles for the two foods; e.g., formal (*shin*) and "grass" (*sō*), or running (*gyō*) and "grass" (*sō*).

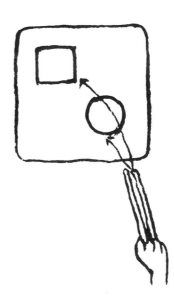

Fig. 23. Foods should always be arranged so they can be eaten easily. Avoid the arrangement above, which forces the server (or diner) to cross over one food to reach the other.

16. Three sashimi arrangements (from top)

ARRANGEMENT: flat style
FOOD: sea bream; garnishes: fern fiddleheads, *wasabi* horseradish
Rectangular dish, Imari porcelain, bamboo design.

ARRANGEMENT: piled-up style
FOOD: sea bream; garnishes: *wasabi* horseradish, *iwatake*, rape blossoms
Plate, Imari porcelain, Shinto banner design.

ARRANGEMENT: cedar-tree style
FOOD: sea bream; garnishes: *wasabi* horseradish, *iwatake*
Rectangular dish, Imari porcelain.

Three-Variety Scattered Style

When three varieties of food are served in one square, flat dish, a strict arrangement of equal amounts set in an equilateral triangle is extremely rigid and formal; besides, that way there is no room to set serving chopsticks. Instead, the three varieties are divided into "main," "subordinate," and "side," the main item being largest in quantity and the side item smallest. They should be laid in a scalene triangle with the main item at the apex. Again, each dish should not be arranged in the same style; variety, as always, is the goal.

Similarly, in a rectangular dish, three items of food laid in an evenly spaced row results in an uninteresting, childish appearance. Again the three are divided into main, secondary, and side dishes, with the side dish, which is smallest, placed between the others—not centered, but next to either the main or the secondary dish. The irregularity of the space thus created adds a pleasing rhythm and grace.

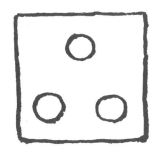

Fig. 24. Avoid uninteresting equilateral triangles.

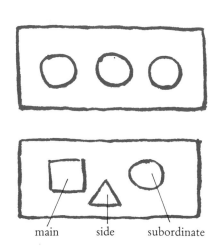

main   side   subordinate

Fig. 26. A straight line of food on a rectangular dish is uninteresting. Change the balance by moving the side food closer to the main food.

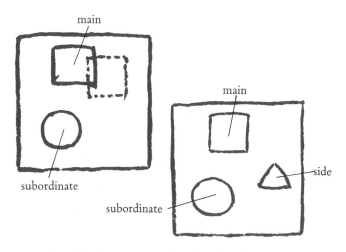

Fig. 25. The three-variety style is based on the two-variety. Shift the main food a bit back and to the left and add the side in the space created.

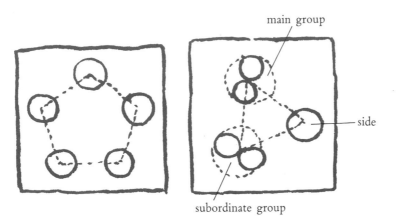

main group

side

subordinate group

Fig. 27. No matter how many elements are added, a regular, symmetrical pattern is boring. Create a main group and a subordinate group and arrange as you would with the three-variety style.

Five-Variety Scattered Style

When five varieties of food are placed in one serving dish, again an evenly spaced geometric arrangement is considered lacking in sophistication. The five are combined in three groups, which are then arranged in a triangle on the principles described above. The main and secondary groups each have two kinds of food, and the side group—in the upper right—consists of a single food in slightly larger proportion. Each of the three points of the triangle should differ in size and in style of arrangement.

The key to the scattered style of arrangement is the use of space. To demonstrate this, I experimented by putting an identical arrangement of identical foods in three different receptacles: a simple square tray of black lacquer, a round confection tray of black and red lacquer, and a Western utensil of the same size.

In the black lacquer tray, there is ample space, giving the arrangement a bold and imposing appearance; the space so formed is not, indeed, mere emptiness, but a vehicle for the beauty of the vessel itself. In the round tray, the warmth of the surrounding red lacquer enfolds and embraces the arrangement. In the Western style dish, the surface of the ware seemed relatively lacking in interest, so I added a single bamboo leaf. Such leaves have an amazing power to set off food. Their use can be overdone, but in cases like this, both food and dish are enhanced.

17. Arrangements on serving dishes (from top)
ARRANGEMENT: three-ingredient nestled style
FOOD (*takiawase*): simmered shrimp, *yuba* (soybean milk skin),
rape blossoms
Plate by Shōji Hamada.

ARRANGEMENT: rice-bale style
FOOD: omelette rolls stuffed with eel
Plate, Mashiko ware, stripe pattern.

ARRANGEMENT: three-ingredient nestled style
FOOD (pickles): *takuan*, turnip leaves and stalks
Bowl, Bizen ware style, incised stripe pattern, by Rosanjin
Kitaōji.

18–20. Five-variety scattered style arrangements in three vessels using identical ingredients

FOOD: (clockwise from left) deep-fried baby sea bream and *tara* (angelica tree) buds; *udo* (*Aralia cordata*) wrapped in soybean milk skin (*yuba*) and shrimp; parboiled *yomena* leaves and field horsetail (*tsukushi*) in sesami paste

VESSELS: (from top) square black lacquer board; lacquer tray; Dansk plate and bamboo grass leaf.

TYPES AND FUNCTIONS OF VESSELS IN *KAISEKI* CUISINE

Summer heat and winter cold, separated by the mildness of spring and autumn, each season giving way to the next in an endless circle marked by endless subtle shifts—in a country blessed with sharply distinct seasons, nowhere is this rich seasonal interplay and variation more apparent than in the ancient capital of Kyoto. Here, drawn by the purity of the water, numerous devotees of the tea ceremony established themselves, and here, amid the abundance of nature, an elegant style of cooking associated with the tea ceremony was developed, known as *kaiseki* cuisine.

Kaiseki is only one among many styles of Japanese cooking, but undoubtedly it is the most refined. With the appearance in the Muromachi period of *wabi* tea, the tea cult that repudiated ostentatious displays in favor of the beauty of austerity, *kaiseki* developed slowly, polished and brought to perfection by the superlative aesthetic sense of the tea masters.

Kaiseki food is served as a prelude to the tea ceremony. Formerly Zen monks ate only twice daily, in the morning and again at noon, and to endure the pangs of hunger they would insert a heated stone in the folds of their robe; hence the word *kaiseki*, written with characters for "breast" and "stone." The thick tea of the tea ceremony is less palatable on an empty stomach, so it is accompanied by just enough food to stave off hunger—this is the origin and meaning of *kaiseki* cuisine.

Kaiseki food is characterized by a number of features related to the fact that the meal is not of prime importance in itself but serves merely as a preliminary to tea. For example, great emphasis is laid in the tea cult on respect for nature and the seasons, so *kaiseki* meals use only fresh, seasonal foods. Extremely light seasoning is used to avoid detracting from the natural flavor inherent in each ingredient. There are limits, too, on the number of dishes that may be served, and the size of a serving must never exceed what a person can comfortably eat at one sitting.

The basic formula for a *kaiseki* meal is *ichijū issai* or "soup and one"—meaning, in addition to rice, a meal consists of a bowl of *miso* soup and something served in a *mukōzuke* dish, consisting usually of fresh, uncooked fish. The *ichijū nisai*, "soup and two," formula adds a dish of simmered foods (*wanmori* or *nimono wan*), and the *ichijū sansai*, "soup and three," formula, adds a grilled food (*yakimono*) to the "soup and two." The meal invariably ends with a very light soup called *hashiarai* (literally, "chopstick wash"), *hassun*, pickles, and green tea. Today "soup and three" is the standard menu; on festive occasions, or when desired, a plate or two of *shiizakana*, small delicacies to accompany saké, may be passed among the guests as well.

Various rules prescribe how *kaiseki* dishes should be served. Above all, a sense of timing is crucial. The host must see that hot foods and cold foods are served at the proper temperatures, in properly heated or chilled receptacles; their arrivals must be spaced to match the guests' progress, neither rushing nor delaying the tempo of the meal.

Taste, while naturally important, is by no means the only consideration. Equally important is the appearance of the food in its dish, a small tableau of form and color. Since the meal is in principle hand-prepared by the host, it need not, however, be elaborate. In fact a showy, intricate arrangement that calls undue attention to itself is out of keeping with the spirit of *kaiseki* food, which must be served with all naturalness, simplicity, and freshness.

Kaiseki serving dishes include sets of matching vermilion or black lacquer ware called *kaigu*. Vermilion *kaigu* is used for vegetarian fare and black for ordinary occasions. One set comprises the following: an *oshiki* tray, a rice bowl, a soup bowl, saké cups, a *haidai* (a base or stand for saké cups), a pitcher, a rectangular tray, and a round tray. *Mukōzuke*, meanwhile, are round dishes of vermilion lacquer called *chatsu* or *rutsu*. Vermilion lacquer *kaigu*, everyday eating utensils at Zen temples, are made by priests as part of their religious discipline.

Despite the virtues of convenience and harmony, however, *kaigu* tend to be monotonous and dull. For greater variety, it became acceptable to mix wares of many kinds—china, wood, bamboo, metal, glass (with lacquer ware still dominant)—to create a sense of newness and surprise. If *kaigu* exemplifies the beauty of harmony, then such admixtures exemplify the beauty of contrast.

How to combine wares is a complex question to be settled differently on different occasions. A number of conditions must be taken into account, including the theme of the occasion, the season, the setting and its atmosphere, the menu, and the ages and tastes of the guests. No two bowls of the same shape or style must ever be used in succession; at the same time there must be an overall impression of unified, harmonious beauty.

Hosting a *kaiseki* meal, and the tea ceremony that follows, is undoubtedly a great deal of work, with endless details to be handled in the preparations as well as the actual staging of the event. Yet despite the many demands on the host, a saying has it that "the host's pleasure is seven parts, the guests' pleasure three." That is, tea is a highly creative pastime, satisfying on multiple levels, and so the many tasks it requires are not seen as fussy chores but as an elevated form of entertainment.

First one decides on the menu and then chooses appropriate wares, taking care to avoid duplication. A skillful choice of wares is predicated on exact knowledge of their various characteristics, with special reference to the season at hand. Tea adepts divide the year in two main parts, from May through October, when the small charcoal brazier (*furo*) is used, and from November through April, when the hearth is used. Sensitivity to the seasons being of paramount importance, care is taken with utensils—as with all else—to strive for an impression of coolness in summer and warmth in winter. When the brazier is out, shallow wares of light, refreshing colors are used, such as celadon or white porcelain and glass, while in the hearth season, deeper utensils of soft warmth are favored, such as Shino and Oribe wares.

Interestingly, vessels of Bizen, Iga, Shigaraki, Tamba, and certain other wares seem either warm or cool, depending on how they are used. Filled briefly with hot water in winter, they retain enough heat to keep food hot, without becoming uncomfortably hot to the touch like porcelain. Chilled with ice water in summer, they take on a cool and refreshing air; food of any color can be arranged in them to superb effect, enhanced by the moist freshness of the surrounding space.

There is also a practical reason for soaking a ceramic vessel in cold or hot water before using: when such a vessel is used dry, food juices and odors penetrate it, spoiling it for future use. After using, such wares are always set out to air for a day or two to dry them completely: if this is not done, they are apt to become moldy in Japan's high humidity.

In any case, summer vessels of porcelain are cool but lack softness, while in winter, stoneware is warm but heavy. Therefore in both seasons a mixture is preferred; generally hot food is served in heat-retentive stoneware, while *mukōzuke* and other cold dishes may be served in either stoneware or porcelain, whichever better suits the overall design.

Hassun trays are almost always made of plain, unadorned Japanese cedar. Like stoneware vessels, they (and chopsticks) are set in water before using to close the pores and prevent juices from seeping in; the freshness of the moist, straight-grained wood lends dignity to any food arrangement.

Lacquer ware is appropriate in all seasons. It brings out the colors of foods and adds a look of profundity. The sight of pure white rice in a bowl of vermilion or black lacquer is at once exquisitely beautiful and enticing.

Properly used, utensils take on life. The simplicity of a tea room calls for simple utensils, while elegant utensils are suited rather to the dignity of a drawing room or a spacious hall. And yet after a succession of simple, austere wares, the vivid elegance of a saké bottle decorated with graceful brushwork in red comes as a relief, allowing everyone to relax. A meal in which fine pieces are used sparingly, mixed occasionally with simple wares, leaves a far more lasting impression than a display of unrelieved ostentation.

Finally, I would like to follow the roles of utensils and foods through the successive courses of a *kaiseki* meal.

New Year *Kaiseki*

Preliminaries—*Kumidashi*

The *kaiseki* meal about to begin is part of *hatsugama*, the first tea ceremony of the new year. In keeping with the festivity of the occasion, it is presented with an extra touch of gaiety. The meal, a fairly substantial one prepared by the host, begins at noon, and is followed by *matcha*, the delicately bitter tea of the tea ceremony itself.

Promptly at 12:00 the guests arrive and are shown to a waiting room (*yoritsuki*). There an assistant brings them *kōsen* (a fragrant hot drink), served in special tea cups on a round wooden tray. The cups used here, called *kumidashi*, are about the size of *soba* noodle sauce cups (see Pl. 125).

Plain hot water may also be served; for this occasion, the host has added a bit of pickled orchid to each cup.

The sole decoration in the meticulously cleaned room is a hanging scroll that expresses the theme of the gathering. The Japanese preference for simplicity is well expressed in the decor; if the scroll painting is a particularly fine one, then even flowers are considered unnecessary. The painting is allowed to say everything, and all nonessentials are omitted in a style of extreme abbreviation.

Soon the guests move on to outdoor seats in the garden, where, to celebrate the new year, the old bamboo in the surrounding fence and elsewhere has all been replaced with fresh-cut green bamboo. While waiting in these refreshing surroundings, the guests enter slowly into the mood of the occasion. Before long the host appears, and after an exchange of silent bows they move together through the garden, absorbing its wintry aspect before entering finally into the teahouse. Here, as they quietly savor the fragrance from the burning hearthpit, the *kaiseki* begins and proceeds smoothly, flowingly, toward its goal: the enjoyment of a bowl of tea.

21. Waiting room for the tea ceremony (*yoritsuki*).
SCROLL: Plum tree and calligraphy, by Ikkyū Sōjun.
KUMIDASHI: noodle-sauce cups, Imari porcelain, bamboo grass design.
Tray, pine wood, poem and calligraphy by the nun Rengetsu.

First Course—*Oshiki, mukōzuke,* soup bowl, rice bowl, *Rikyū-bashi*

First a tray (*oshiki*) is brought in, with a rice bowl in the left front, a soup bowl in the right front, and a *mukōzuke* dish centered behind them to form the apex of a triangle. The chopsticks are *Rikyū-bashi* of new cedar wood, soaked beforehand in water to make them easier to use. When the tray used has a rim, as here, chopstick rests are dispensed with; instead the chopsticks are laid across the edge, protruding slightly to the left. The rice bowl and soup bowl, together with their lids, form a set of four nested bowls. After the lids are removed, they are placed rim to rim beside the tray, on the tatami mats; they may be used as receptacles for food passed around later in the meal.

The *mukōzuke* dish, too, may be used as a receptacle for other foods or pickles. Since it remains in place throughout the meal, always in the guest's eye, it must be suited to the theme and tenor of the gathering. The Shino ware used here has a warmth and substance appropriate to the time of year. Its irregular shape and rough texture also relieve the formality of the geometric shapes and arrangement of the tray and bowls.

The rice (*meshi*) is laid in a glistening white line across the bottom of a black lacquer bowl. It is a mere mouthful or two, the host's way of saying "Here is a taste of the just-cooked rice. I hope this will do until the meal is ready." The soup (*misoshiru*) is also small in amount, decorated with two bright azuki beans to add to the holiday atmosphere. Guests partake alternately of soup and rice, placing the bowls in the palm of the left hand as they do so. Since saké will shortly appear, this first course serves also to prevent guests from taking an alcoholic beverage on an empty stomach. The *mukōzuke* is stirred well and eaten after the saké has been brought out and after suitable admiration of its quietly tasteful arrangement.

22. *Oshiki* tray, black lacquer.
Mukōzuke dish, Shino ware.
ARRANGEMENT: piled-up style
FOOD: sea bream sashimi, day lily (*kanzō*) stems, *iwatake*

Four nested bowls, black lacquer, Rikyū style.
FOOD: rice; miso soup with *ebi-imo* yam cut in tortoiseshell (hexagonal) pattern, azuki beans, and mustard
Rikyū-bashi chopsticks

Second Course—*Kannabe, haidai, sakazuki, wanmori*

Next, after making sure that the guests have finished their soup, the host brings out a saké server (*kannabe*) and a lacquer stand (*haidai*) on which are stacked vermilion-lacquer saké cups (*sakazuki*), one for each member of the gathering. He then goes from guest to guest, offering saké to each one. The bright cloisonné lid on the server and the *maki-e* lacquer design on the stand, both suited to the New Year, add a touch of festivity. Each guest takes a saké cup and holds it out for the host to fill with heated wine. In *kaiseki*, saké conveys the hospitality of the host and his desire for guests to relax and enjoy their food to the full. The amount drunk is small, not enough to cause inebriation.

After this, the host reenters with a round serving tray on which sits a larger, lidded lacquer bowl beautifully decorated with gold *maki-e*. This is the *wanmori* course. The guest picks up the *wanmori* bowl in

23. Saké server (*kannabe*), floral lozenge and grass pattern (and cloisonné lid), by Kojōmi.
Stand (*haidai*), *maki-e* on black lacquer, New Year's design, by Sano Chōkan.
Saké cups, Negoro lacquer.

Lidded bowl, *maki-e* lacquer, camellia design.
ARRANGEMENT: bowl style
FOOD: thick clear soup with shrimp, *yuzu* citron, carrot, lettuce hearts, and oyster mushrooms

his left hand and removes the lid; in the same moment a subtle, delicious fragrance of *yuzu* citron fills the air, and a rich assortment of colors—white of shrimp, yellow of citron, green, red, and brown of vegetables—greets the eye. The clear broth is filled with abundant ingredients, moreover, satisfying one's hunger as well. *Wanmori* is designed to appeal to the guest in a variety of ways; it is the center and highlight of the meal. It is followed by a second round of drinks from the *kannabe*.

Third Course—*Yakimono, meshitsugi*

Following quickly on the *wanmori* is *yakimono*—grilled or broiled seafood prepared directly over a flame. As with all fish served in *kaiseki*, the bones are entirely removed. Here, five servings of broiled fish (one per guest) have been arranged in a square dish of Oribe ware, with careful attention to the disposition of surrounding space. A pair of green bamboo serving chopsticks lies diagonally across the front of the dish. The food is arranged in piled-up style (*kasanemori*) to allow guests to help themselves easily and to keep the food from getting cold. The dish itself is pleasantly warm to the touch, in testimony to the host's desire for his guests to enjoy the food while it is hot.

Next to appear is a large rice container (*meshitsugi*) on top of which is a round serving tray (*kayoibon*) bearing a rice paddle (*meshi-jakushi*). This the host leaves in the room, so that the group may freely help themselves as many times as they like. Extra soup is also brought out on a serving tray. The texture and taste of rice change according to the length of time it is steamed, so by serving rice twice—once before the *wanmori* course and again now—the host allows his guests to enjoy an extra dimension of flavor.

24. Square dish, Oribe ware, pine tree design.
ARRANGEMENT: piled-up style
FOOD: grilled pompano
Green bamboo serving chopsticks

Covered rice container, round tray, and rice paddle, black lacquer.

Fourth Course—*Azuke-bachi* (two kinds), *azuke-tokkuri, guinomi*

The elegant decorated bowl shaped like a Chinese bellflower forms a bright and pleasing contrast with the rather heavy, formal style of the preceding lacquer, Shino, and Oribe wares, all in circles and squares. The porcelain bowl goes well with the vinegar-dressed foods (*sunomono*) arranged in it.

Following this is a round bowl of Kiseto ware, containing a stewlike dish called *takiawase* ("simmered together"). The soft serenity of this vessel contrasts strikingly in shape, color, and texture with the flower-shaped bowl beside it, each emphasizing the good points of the other.

Now the host departs, leaving his guests with these dishes and with a large stoneware saké bottle (*tokkuri*) and a selection of stoneware cups (*guinomi*). In his absence, the guests help themselves to the food before them, sharing quiet conversation.

If the *wanmori* course gives substance to *kaiseki*, *yakimono* and *shiizakana* give it depth. *Shiizakana* is served not only with meals of "one and three" (*ichijū sansai*; i.e., a bowl of soup and three side dishes), but on

25. Chinese bellflower-shaped bowl, Kakiemon style porcelain.
ARRANGEMENT: jumbled style
FOOD: vinegared crab, *suizenji nori*; garnish: bōfū

Bowl, Kiseto ware style, by Rosanjin Kitaōji.
ARRANGEMENT: two-ingredient nestled style
FOOD : simmered turnips, shrimp, *yuzu* citron zest slivers
Green bamboo serving chopsticks

Saké bottle, Bizen ware.
Hexagonal saké cup.

any special occasion or whenever the host may choose, as extra dishes or accompaniments to saké. Since the bowls containing the foods and the saké bottle are deposited with the guests, they are also known as *azuke-tokkuri* and *azuke-bachi* (*azuke* from the verb *azukeru*, "to entrust with"; *bachi* means bowl).

Yet from an excess of desire to please one's guests, it will not do to prepare too many dishes or to offer more food than can comfortably be eaten. If the guest is left feeling "Ah, that was good. I wish there had been more," then the memory of the meal and its various flavors will not easily leave him; but if so much food is pushed on him that he cannot eat any more, his memory of the meal will quickly vanish.

Fifth Course—*Hashiarai, kannabe, hassun*

The host returns and passes around small, delicate bowls on a round tray. Despite its name, the purpose of *hashiarai* ("chopstick wash") is not to wash one's chopsticks but to rinse and refresh one's mouth after eating and to signify the essential completion of the meal. It has the further purpose of preparing the guests for the ritual saké to follow. The liquid in the bowls is a small amount of hot water with just the barest tang of kelp. Of all the foods served in *kaiseki*, none is so simple and none perhaps so effective: it purifies the senses and clarifies the rhythm of the meal, deepening one's pleasure in the richer flavors that follow and precede.

The host next brings out the *hassun* tray in his left hand, the saké server in his right; this is the third round of drinks, and exchange of cups between guest and host. The saké server is the same as before, but the lid has been changed to one of Oribe ware, for a new impression—one that blends well with the *hassun* tray.

The *hassun* course is served in the spirit of a modest afterthought, as if the host was saying, "Really this

26. Small covered lacquer bowl with flared lip by Sōtetsu I. FOOD: thin, clear stock with pickled plum (*umeboshi*) and butterbur (*fuki*) bud

Saké server (*kannabe*), floral lozenge and grass pattern (and Oribe ware lid), by Kojōmi.

Hassun tray, cedar wood.
ARRANGEMENT: scattered style
FOOD: tiny green pickled daikon radish (arranged in rice-bale style); mullet roe (arranged in piled-up style)
Green bamboo serving chopsticks

was a meager sort of meal, but now, if you don't mind, would you care to join me for one last drink and a small bite to go with it?" At this point to bring out some fine ceramic ware would seem like showing off. It was, I am sure, a tea master sensitive to the beauty of everyday wooden utensils, the sort used unthinkingly by ordinary people, who thought of and designed the square tray of unpainted Japanese cedar known as *hassun*. A tray of unpretentious sophistication, it is suitable for the most formal entertaining. Served wet and gleaming, its moisture accenting the beauty of its cedar grain, it bears "something from the sea" (fish, shellfish) and

"something from the land" (a vegetable dish), spaced at a carefully calculated distance from one another.

While serving the food to each guest in turn, one piece at a time, the host also exchanges saké cups with each person. This is the sole time during the meal when host and guest can chat in close, relaxed communication.

For the *hassun* course alone, ingredients slightly ahead of season are used. In February, for example, one may include a tiny serving of preserved *tsukushi* (field horsetails; a spring plant) to stimulate the imagination and invest the coming of spring with that much more anticipation. In this way, the guest at *kaiseki* can relish not only the various flavors of the meal itself but also the fine subtleties of its planning.

Sixth Course—*Yutō, kōnomono*

This course marks the finish of the meal. The host brings in a rectangular tray on which sit a bowl, a lacquer ewer (*yutō*), and a dipper (*yunoko sukui*). Inside the *yutō* is hot water tasting just slightly of salt and bits of savory scorched rice, golden-brown in hue, called *yunoko*. The lid of the *yutō* is removed, and the *yunoko*

27. Hot water ewer, dipper, and rectangular tray, black lacquer.
FOOD: hot water and *yunoko* scorched rice

Small bowl, Iga ware.
ARRANGEMENT: three-ingredient nestled style
FOOD: pickled sliced turnip stems rolled in thin pickled turnip (or daikon) slices, turnip greens, *takuan* daikon pickles
Green bamboo serving chopsticks

are taken out with the dipper and put into a bowl; then hot water is poured over them from the spout.

The *kōbachi*, or bowl containing *kōnomono* (pickles), is the last vessel to be used in the meal; usually a dish of some character and dignity is chosen, to end the meal on a strong note. The *kōnomono* itself is always pickled radish (*takuan*), year round, with one seasonal accompaniment. The radish is scored finely on the back with a knife so that it yields readily to the teeth.

After the guests have finished they wipe their dishes clean and replace the lids on their bowls. When all is ready, everyone simultaneously drops his chopsticks lightly onto his tray as a signal to the host, waiting outside the doorway, that the meal is over. Then all the wares and trays are cleared away.

Tea—fuchidaka (omogashi), bon (higashi), teabowl

The assistant places one soft sweet in each of five deep boxes (*fuchidaka*) and brings these in piled in a stack. The guests pass the boxes around, each taking out his or her sweet on paper brought for the occasion; each sweet comes with a small wooden pick, as shown. The *fuchidaka*, with its roomy interior allowing wide margins of space, is the most formal container for sweets.

The *higashibon*, an unlidded container for "dried" confections, may be of any shape; assorted hard confections are placed on it, with careful attention to spacing. Both the hard and soft sweets carry on the New Year's theme in their design.

Finally the guests leave the tea room. They slip into the garden, washing their hands and rinsing their mouths with water from the stone basin to remove the last vestiges of sweetness, which might interfere with their appreciation of the tea yet to come. At last they return to sip the tea prepared before them by their host. The beautiful shape of the teabowl, the pleasurable feel of it in their hands, and its color, harmonizing with

28. Box (*fuchidaka*), black lacquer.
FOOD: sweet bean paste (soft) confection

Tray, green lacquer, gold scroll pattern, by Ōko.
ARRANGEMENT: three-variety scattered style
FOOD: "dried" (hard) confections—plum blossom, pine needle, and *noshi* banner shapes

TEABOWL: Okugōrai type (a type of Karatsu ware).

the green of the whipped tea, all combine to heighten the sensation of taste. So ends the tea gathering.

In *kaiseki* meals, as we have seen, guests' appreciation is directed at the total ambience of the event, an amalgam of overlapping impressions from many sources: the food, the utensils, and their mutual balance and interplay; the use of empty space as a living component of each food arrangement; and the surrounding decor, including hanging scroll, architectural design, and garden layout. Guests must depart feeling happily that food and tea alike were delicious, that the event was enjoyable and wholly in keeping with the spirit of the New Year. Ideally the event should leave lingering vibrations in the mind and senses, such that each guest will long to be invited back again.

III

FUNCTION
AND
BEAUTY

盌
Wan

Bowls (*wan*)   **Plates 29–38**

The bowl, as a container for rice, soups, and stews has been highly developed in Japan. Its basic size and shape, suitable for holding in one hand, have remained fairly constant. The diameter is roughly 12 centimeters, a handy size for grasping between index finger and thumb.

The oldest surviving bowls are from the Yayoi period and were apparently made on a potter's wheel. These were followed by a more durable type—wooden bowls coated with layers of lacquer. Such bowls have the advantage of retaining heat without transmitting it to the fingers. Dried lacquer also resists acid, alkali, salt, alcohol, and other substances, and is both moisture-proof and decay-proof. For these reasons, lacquered bowls were favored by the Japanese for centuries.

The Shōsō-in repository contains fourteen black lacquered bowls from the eighth century. Fairly small in size (10.0 cm. in diameter, 5.0 cm. high), they are well rounded and have a high foot. They are entirely of black lacquer; red lacquer did not come into use until the Heian period and was reserved for the highest nobility.

On the Korean peninsula, slightly larger metal bowls were used; these are normally left on the table rather than picked up and are used with spoons. In the Nara and Heian periods, metal bowls, chopsticks, and spoons were used in Japan as well, among priests and aristocrats, but their use never spread to the populace, and in time they were replaced by wooden ones.

The Japanese art of *maki-e* (gold- and silver-decorated lacquer), which developed from Heian through Muromachi times, was used to embellish bowls, trays, and other eating implements. Nested bowls appeared from the Muromachi period on.

The Meigetsu-in in Kamakura possesses a collection of beautiful red-lacquered bowls inlaid with mother-of-pearl in a pattern of cherry blossoms (Pl. 37). One hundred such bowls were reportedly donated to the temple by the tea master Oda Urakusai (d. 1621).

In the Edo period (1615–1868), sets of dishes owned by feudal lords grew increasingly elaborate, with all manner of new types of eating and drinking vessels. Affluent townsmen copied these for their own use, and gradually, in simplified form, they filtered down to the common people. Distinctive bowls decorated with brief, flowing lacquer paintings were made in each region; among the most famous are those of Yoshino (Pl. 32) and the Hidehira (Pl. 35) type of northeastern Honshu.

Teabowls, tea cups, and rice bowls (*chawan*)
Plates 39–49

Today the term *chawan* denotes three distinct types of ceramic vessels: teabowls for the tea ceremony; *yunomi*, cups for ordinary green tea; and *meshi chawan*, rice bowls. The first, used to drink whisked, powdered tea (*matcha*) in the tea ceremony, is larger than and considerably different in nature from everyday cups and bowls.

Tea was introduced to Japan by the priest Yōsai (1141–1215), who brought it back with him after a sojourn in China. Until about the fifteenth century, it was drunk from Chinese bowls called *tenmoku chawan*. With the rise of the *wabi* tea ceremony in the late Muromachi period, Korean bowls came into high favor; a southern variety called *Ido* in Japan came to be particularly prized. However, *Ido* bowls were not designed expressly for tea. In Korea, they were just ordinary rice bowls. Japanese tea adepts began using them for their own purposes, seeing in such everyday utensils a simple beauty well suited to the ideals of the tea ceremony.

Before long many superb teabowls were being produced in Japan as well, including the red and black Raku bowls, Seto, Oribe, Shino, and other wares of the Momoyama period (Pls. 39–41). In the seventeenth century, Ninsei and other master potters produced elegant teabowls with colorful enameled designs.

Yunomi chawan, generally cylindrical in shape, are used to drink brewed tea such as *bancha* (coarse tea) and *sencha* (high-quality leaf tea) (Pls. 42–44).

The term *meshi chawan* ("rice teabowl") (Pls. 45–49)

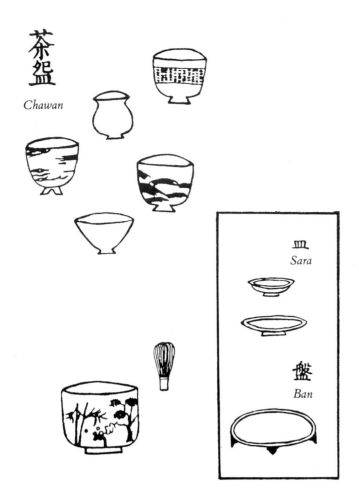

茶盌

Chawan

皿
Sara

盤
Ban

鉢

Hachi

has an interesting history. From ancient times, rice bowls used on formal occasions were made of lacquered wood. In the early Edo period, however, porcelain bowls began to be manufactured in Hizen (northern Kyushu). The name *chawan* was given to these, distinguishing them from the lacquered bowls. Today the switchover to ceramic rice bowls is virtually complete, but the label *chawan* has stuck.

Shallow dishes, plates, and platters (*sara, ban*)
Plates 50–68

In early times a leaf often served as a dish, as can be seen from this poem in the *Man'yōshū*:

> When I am at home
> I heap my rice in an earthen dish;
> Now, on a journey far,
> Grass for my pillow,
> I heap it on an oak leaf.

Shallow dishes or plates (*sara*) were made in Japan in the late Jōmon period, several centuries before Christ. From about A.D. 400, in the Tumulus period, unglazed dishes known as *kawarake* occupied a central position among eating utensils. In the eighth century, a new type of *sara* appeared, called *ban*. Made of many different materials, *ban* were used not only to serve cooked foods and sweets, but also at times as bases for bowls.

Sara similar in usage and appearance to plates of today were first manufactured in the Momoyama period, when the rise of the tea cult led to a heightened demand for pottery.

When the manufacture of blue-and-white porcelain began in Arita in Edo times, eating utensils entered the age of porcelain.

The distinction between *sara* and *hachi* (bowl) is often fuzzy. Large pieces may be called either *sara* or *hirabachi* (shallow bowl), while smaller pieces tend to be confused with both *wan* and *hachi*. There is no clear demarcation among the three. Custom and usage often determine which term is used rather than physical attributes. Further, these Japanese terms are not quite the same as the corresponding English words, making caution necessary in translation.

Bowls, serving bowls, pouring bowls (*hachi, katakuchi*)
Plates 69–77

The word *hachi* derives from the Sanskrit word *patra*, written in Japanese with characters pronounced *hachitara*, eventually shortened to *hachi*. Another name for *hachi* was *ōryō-ki*, used for the begging bowls of mendicant monks, evidence that *hachi* are intimately associated with Buddhism.

Hachi are basically circular, but a number of other shapes are also made, including square, octagonal, flared, and foliate; others have a tall foot (*daibachi*) or a tall body (*dorabachi*). They are made of metal, wood, lacquer, glass, and above all, ceramics.

Hachi with a pouring spout are called *katakuchi* and are made of both lacquer and porcelain; soy sauce, vinegar, saké, and other liquids are emptied into them from kegs, then poured into other, smaller containers. Most are everyday utensils, but occasionally they are used in the tea ceremony.

The term *hachi* can also denote the container in which steamed rice is carried from kitchen to table.

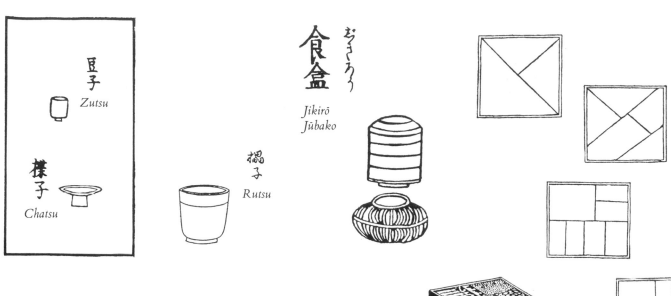

豆子
Zutsu

様子
Chatsu

食盒
おきゝろう

Jikirō
Jūbako

揭子
Rutsu

Mukōzuke dishes (*mukōzuke*)   **Plates 78–96**

Kaiseki ryōri, having originated in Zen temples, at first used only vessels found in such religious institutions. Everything was vermilion lacquered, including trays, bowls, and the dishes called *chatsu*. *Chatsu* are small, shallow, round dishes with a tall foot, used originally for *namasu* (vinegared raw fish and vegetables). Today they are no longer used at everyday meals and survive only for formal tea ceremony cuisine, although at one time they were evidently quite popular, as may be seen in Saikaku's *Kōshoku gonin onna* ("Five Women Who Loved Love"), published in 1686. In later years they were gradually replaced by porcelain dishes; the name was changed to *mukōzuke*, and they were used to hold *sashimi*, vinegar-dressed foods, boiled and seasoned vegetables, and the like.

Mukōzuke now refers to one of the three vessels placed in a triangle on the square tray for one course of the tea ceremony meal. In the left front corner is a rice bowl, in the right front corner a soup bowl, and in the rear, at the apex of the triangle, is the dish called, logically, "far dish" or *mukōzuke* (sometimes abbreviated simply to *mukō*, "far"). It is generally of medium size or smaller, and may be any one of a wide variety of shapes and depths. Representative of tea ceremony cuisine, they vary according to the season, and tea adepts use all their ingenuity in choosing something appropriate.

From Kamakura times through Muromachi, an enormous amount of Chinese porcelain entered Japan. By late Muromachi, many bowls, dishes, plates, and other vessels influenced by Chinese porcelain were being produced in kilns throughout the eastern Mino area. In the Momoyama period, the popularity of the tea ceremony created a soaring interest in pottery, with the result that many completely new ceramic forms came into existence. These wares—Kiseto, Shino, and Oribe—possessed an abundant diversity and originality of style, shape, and design and were (and still are) a source of fresh inspiration for lovers of beauty.

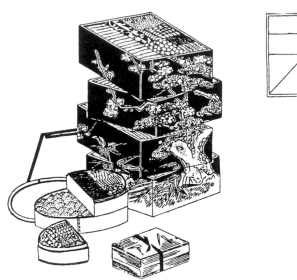

Covered food containers, tiered food boxes, picnic boxes (*jikirō*, *jūbako*, *sagejū*)   **Plates 97–99**

The first documented mention of *jikirō*, lidded food containers, is in 1444. It is believed that in ancient times *jikirō* were lidded bamboo baskets.

Jūbako are made by piling thin cypress boxes in tiers (Pls. 98, 99). Their earliest mention occurs in the early sixteenth century.

In banquet-scene paintings from the Kan'ei era through the Genroku era (1624–1704), *jūbako* are often depicted. After that they fade from use, being replaced in the Hōei era (1704–10) by *suzuri-buta* (lids of inkstone boxes), *hachi*, and *sara*. Henceforth *jūbako* were used only at New Year; to this day, an assortment of special foods called *osechi ryōri* is served on New Year's Day, beautifully arranged in *jūbako*.

With a revival of the Doll Festival (*hina-matsuri*) in the mid-eighteenth century, a related form of box, the *sagejū*, became popular as a portable picnic set for pleasure trips. *Sagejū* hold saké bottles, cups, and a set of small serving dishes, all of which fit handily inside a frame with a handle (Pl. 97). In late Edo many lovely *sagejū* were made and were popular for boating excursions and picnics.

行厨
Bentō

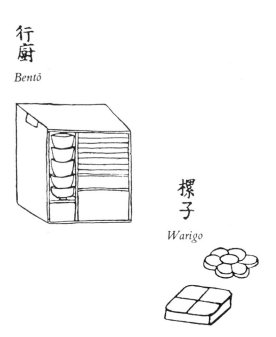

楪子
Warigo

銚子
Chōshi

偏提
Hisage

鏇
*Ashinabe
Kannabe*

Containers for box lunches (*warigo, ori, bentō*)

The term *warigo*, which first appears in the Heian period, refers to a container made of thin sheets of cypress wood with compartments for rice and various side dishes. *Warigo* were generally lidded and made in a variety of shapes, including cylindrical, square, rectangular, triangular, fan-shaped, and foliate. They were also called *mentsū, mempa,* and *wappa.* Simple wicker baskets (*kōri*) made of willow and bamboo, designed to be thrown away after one use, were also favored.

Containers for box lunches sold at stations and recreation centers today are called *ori* (from *oru,* to bend or fold) because they were originally made by bending thin sheets of wood into a box shape. The lid is tied on with cords. *Ori* are also used for gifts and souvenirs.

A popular container in modern times is *shōkadō bentō,* a thirty-centimeter-square lacquered box divided into four equal compartments containing an entire *kaiseki ryōri* meal.

Hot water ewers (*yutō, yutsugi*)   Plates 100, 101

Yutō are cylindrical containers with a spout, lid, and handle, used mainly for carrying hot water from kitchen to table (Pls. 100, 101). In mid-Muromachi times, however, they were used also as saké servers. Most are of lacquered wood, either black or vermilion.

After a tea ceremony meal, small bits of rice scorched a golden brown (*yunoko*) are placed in the hot water inside a *yutō* and are served with a scoop called a *yunoko sukui.* This practice is said to have originated from guests' requests for the crisp, lightly scorched boiled rice at the bottom of the cooking pot, considered a delicacy among Japanese.

Saké servers (*chōshi, hisage, kannabe, chirori*)
Plates 102–106

Chōshi are saké servers used at banquets, with long handles for filling saké cups at a small distance. They are often seen in screen paintings. Originally of copper or brass, later lacquered *chōshi* became common, being especially popular at weddings and other ceremonial occasions. *Ryōguchi* (double-spouted) *chōshi,* designed to be used either to the pourer's right or left, are for very large banquets.

Saké servers shaped sometimes like *yutō,* with a carrying handle attached, are called *hisage.* Most are made of pewter, bronze, and other metals, and like *chōshi* they are used at wedding feasts.

At tea ceremonies, iron saké servers with spouts and

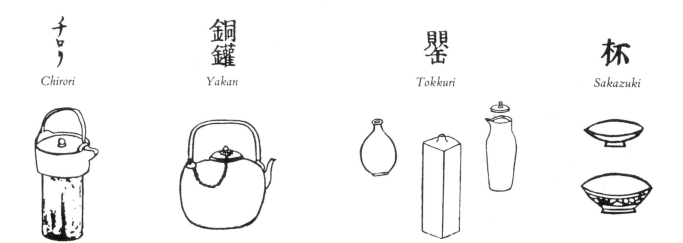

千ロリ
Chirori

銅鑵
Yakan

甖
Tokkuri

杯
Sakazuki

handles are used; these are called *kannabe* or, from the three feet on which some stand, *ashinabe* (foot-pot).

Chirori are saké-heating vessels designed to be set in hot water. Originally they were made of silver, pewter, brass, or other metals, but later ceramic *chirori* became popular. Barrel-shaped, with a carrying handle, they were especially popular in Edo, until replaced by porcelain *tokkuri* (saké bottles). Today, *chōshi* has become a generic term for any saké container.

Teapots, kettles (*dobin, yakan, kyūsu*)   Plate 107

Dobin (teapots) are ceramic vessels used to pour hot water and saké as well as tea. They have a spout, a handle, and a lid. The word *dobin* appears in the *Heiji monogatari* (1180) and other early sources; originally made of iron, they changed to ceramic in the late Muromachi period. In the mid-nineteenth century *dobin* were widely made in Japan, continuing to be in high demand through the Meiji period.

Porcelain *dobin* have been made in Imari (Saga Prefecture), Seto (Aichi Prefecture) and Izushi (Hyōgo Prefecture) since about 1890.

Vessels of the same shape made of copper or brass are called *yakan* (kettles). In scroll paintings like *Ippen hijiri-e* (1299) and *Kasuga gongen kenki* (1309), they are shown used for preparing medicines. Later they were used to boil tea water.

A related utensil is the *kyūsu*, a tiny teapot holding about two servings, with handle, lid, and spout. Tea is poured by grasping the handle, pressing the lid lightly with the right index finger, and bending the wrist. Originating in China for heating saké, the *kyūsu* came to Japan in mid-Edo; with the popularity of brewed tea, they were soon in great demand. *Kyūsu* of master Kyoto potters like Aoki Mokubei (1767–1833) and Okada Kyūta (d. 1832) are particularly famous. There are also fine *kyūsu* among Banko wares in Mie Prefecture, and, from late Edo on, among Tokoname wares as well.

Saké bottles (*tokkuri*)   Plates 108–116

Tokkuri were originally bottles for liquids of all kinds—saké, vinegar, soy sauce—but from the mid-Muromachi period they became saké containers.

Early *tokkuri* were quite large; in Muromachi times, bottles with capacity of a liter (or more) were made. Many resembled scallions or shallots in shape. Depending on their use, place of origin, shape, and color, they are called by a variety of names. One such example are the *funa-dokkuri* ("boat tokkuri," broad-based, large bottles for use on boats; Pl. 109).

The Edo period ceramic saké bottle still was generous in size. With the great activity in ceramic production in the nineteenth century, what are called "poor-man's" *tokkuri* (*bimbō-dokkuri*) were produced in great numbers. These often bore the name of a brewer or saké shop.

Large ceramic *tokkuri* disappearred in the Shōwa period with mass production of glass saké bottles holding one *shō* (1.8 liters). The only vessel bearing the name *tokkuri* today is the small *kan-dokkuri* used for heating saké: it holds one *gō* (1 *gō* = 180 ml) or two *gō*.

Saké cups (*sakazuki*)   Plate 108

The word *sakazuki* had been in use since the age of the *Man'yōshū*. Ancient saké cups were all of unglazed pottery. In the Kamakura period, wooden cups were used, then a foot was added, and eventually lacquer, gold, and silver were used.

According to an illustrated dictionary called *Wakan sansai zu-e* (1712), porcelain cups (also known as *choku*) shaped like morning glories were used for cold saké. Today, cups called *guinomi* are used for tea ceremony cuisine and at restaurants.

Saké cups with a fish design in the bottom are used for festive occasions (page 5), the *tai* (sea bream), a fish associated with celebrations, is an especially popular decoration.

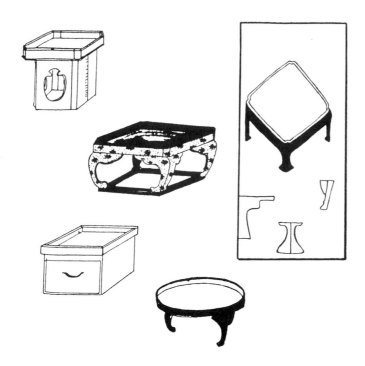

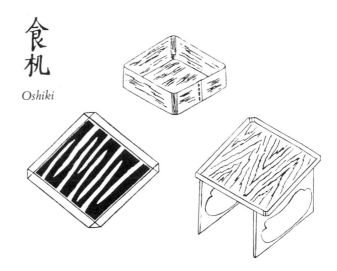

食机
Oshiki

Tray-tables (*daiban, tsuigasane, takatsuki, kakeban, zen*)
Plates 119–124

The history of Japanese tray-tables for dining begins with a large table (*tsukue*) brought over from China. Large ones, (about 2.4 meters across) were called *daiban*; others, roughly half that size, were called *kiri* ("cut") *daiban*.

Takatsuki are round or square low stands with a single leg (Pl. 119).

Tsuigasane are tables used by the nobility, consisting of a square rimmed tray (*oshiki*) set on a four-sided base (Pl. 120). Originally this form was made of plain cypress wood, but from the Kamakura period on, lacquered ones became popular, often decorated with beautiful *maki-e*. Those with decorative holes cut in three sides of the base are called *sanbō*, those with holes in all four sides *yohō*. The latter are generally considered more elegant.

Kakeban, also used exclusively by the nobility, consist of a tray (*oshiki*) attached to a base with four curving legs in a frame (Pl. 121). *Kakeban* and related utensils were decorated with splendid lacquer designs, such as the ones used at a banquet given by Toyotomi Hideyoshi in honor of Tokugawa Ieyasu, which had the Tokugawa hollyhock crest in *maki-e*.

The varieties of tray-tables used by commoners are illustrated in the encyclopedic *Wakan sansai zu-e* (1712) and the *Morisada mankō* (1853) record. Some of the most popular were *chōsoku zen* ("butterfly-leg" tray; Pl. 122), *sōwa zen* (named for a seventeenth century tea master), *nekoashi zen* ("cat's leg" tray), and *kigu zen*, a long-legged tray. *Hako zen*, or *orisuke zen*, a box-shaped structure used for everyday meals by people in Osaka and Kyoto, took its name from samurai servants, although Zen priests used this form as well. The top functions as a lid and table surface; dishes and utensils are stored inside (Pl. 124).

Trays (*bon, oshiki, fuchidaka*)
Plate 123

Bon (also known as *ban* in the early Heian period) are flat trays with shallow rims, usually square or round, with variations such as crescent-moon or plum-blossom shapes. They are usually about thirty-six centimeters in diameter; this is said to correspond roughly to the average hip width of the Japanese people, making it ideal for carrying in two hands, arms bent at the elbow.

Many lovely and distinctive kinds of lacquered trays have been produced in Japan, such as Negoro lacquer and trays decorated with *maki-e*. *Shunkei-nuri* accents the natural beauty of the wood grain: the wood is dyed yellow or red then covered with a layer of transparent lacquer. Still others are named after the color of lacquer used, such as *asagi bon* (light yellow) and *seishitsu bon* (blue). *Kuchiki bon*, from Shiga Prefecture, and *Yoshino bon*, from Nara Prefecture, are examples of trays made in local folk lacquer traditions.

Oshiki are not used to carry food to the table, but rather serve as tables themselves, placed directly on the floor. Ordinary square, rimmed ones are called *hira oshiki* (Pl. 22); among the many variations are ones with corners cut at an angle, *sumikiri oshiki* (Pl. 1).

Fuchidaka are high-rimmed *oshiki*. According to the *Teijō zakki*, published in 1843, those with the corners cut and feet attached were considered the most elegant and were used to serve sweets or cooked foods to guests (Pl. 28).

Various rules of good taste and etiquette govern the use of trays. For example, food is always arranged in a *fuchidaka* with the four corners left empty. Round trays (including those with eight or more sides) must be placed with the seam on the rim facing the guest. Conversely, those of four to seven sides are placed with the seam away from the guest.

Noodle-sauce cups (*soba choko*)
Plate 125

References to buckwheat (*soba*) begin around the eighth century, but buckwheat noodles, now a popular dish, were

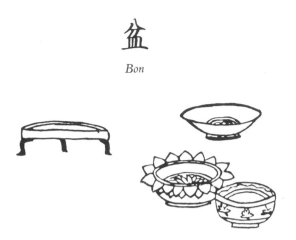

盆

Bon

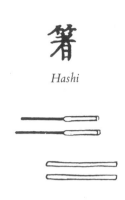

箸

Hashi

not eaten until the 1600s. By 1700 the number of buckwheat noodle shops had grown considerably, and in the late 1800s there were some four thousand in the capital alone. *Soba choko*, which hold the sauce in which *soba* noodles are dipped, were made from the beginning of the eighteenth century. Originally, *choko* referred to a dish used for *mukōzuke* in the tea ceremony; the word applied to the holders for *soba* noodle sauce because of a similarity in shape. Early *soba choko* were of Imari porcelain and had a tall foot. Their simple but elegant decorations, along with their convenient, stackable shape, have made them very popular and flexible everyday utensils.

Chopsticks (*hashi*)

Plate 126

In contrast to the "iron culture" of the West, Japan may be said to have a "wood culture," the prime symbol of which is chopsticks.

Chopsticks are not, of course, uniquely Japanese. Used throughout Asia, they first entered Japan from China via the Korean peninsula. Yet Japan is the only country where traditionally the entire meal is eaten with chopsticks alone. They have developed here on a scale unknown elsewhere, in a wide range of styles and materials.

A passage in the *Wei zhi*, a third-century Chinese chronicle, states "The people of Wa eat with their hands"; from this it would appear that chopsticks had not yet come into use in the Yayoi period. The existence of a tumulus called *Hashizuka*, "Chopstick Mound," however, suggests that they were in use by at least the fifth or sixth century. The earliest recorded mention of them is in the *Kojiki* (*Record of Ancient Matters*; 712); the earliest form, a pincerlike implement still used in imperial rites at Ise Shrine.

Chopsticks have exerted a profound influence on the appearance and style of Japanese cuisine. Designed to pick up food in bite-sized pieces, they are well suited for savoring the aroma, taste, and texture of a dish. Each food must be cut into pieces of chopstick-manageable size before serving. Chopsticks also help to explain the lack in Japanese cuisine of complex sauces and gravies, emphasizing instead the natural flavor of each ingredient.

More than fifty kinds of chopsticks are said to be in use today. Unique to Japan are *sugibashi*, cedar chopsticks. The forested district of Yoshino, in Nara Prefecture, was traditionally a major center for the production of kegs for high-quality saké—and, as a by-product, straight-grained cedar chopsticks. In particular, the kind known as *Rikyū-bashi* (Pls. 22, 126), tapered at both ends and flattened in between, is considered the easiest of all to use and is in high demand for tea ceremony cuisine and the like.

Other kinds of chopsticks are made of various materials. *Toribashi* (serving chopsticks), used in tea ceremony cuisine, are made principally of green or white bamboo; transcending their function as mere tools, they have become objects of aesthetic appreciation in themselves. *Waribashi*, disposable half-split chopsticks, are made primarily of pine. Willow chopsticks, because of their great pliability and durability, are popular for weddings and other auspicious occasions (Pl. 1). Chopsticks used in the home are mostly of lacquered wood, broad at the top and tapered at the bottom.

A number of rules govern the etiquette of chopsticks, some of which are set down in a late Edo period collection of writings by Ise Sadatake published in 1843, entitled *Teijō zakki* ("Miscellaneous Notes"). Taboos dating back to the fifteenth century include those against *saigoshi* (crossing dishes), i.e., reaching with chopsticks beyond a near dish, and *utsuri-bashi* (switching chopsticks), i.e., transferring one's chopsticks directly from one side dish to another without first taking rice.

The use of chopstick rests to keep the food-holding end off the tabletop dates back to Heian times. Eleventh-century documents contain an illustration of a pair of silver crane-shaped chopstick rests, far larger than any used today. On festive occasions, according to *Teijō zakki*, ear-shaped pottery holders were commonly used. Today small rests are made in a wide variety of appealing and imaginative shapes.

73

BOWLS

29. Modern lacquered bowls.

30. Two nested bowls, lacquer and gold leaf, peach design.

31. Two nested bowls, lacquer and gold leaf.

32. Bowl and cover, Yoshino lacquer.

33. Three nested bowls, lacquer and gold leaf, paulownia design.

34. Three nested bowls, lacquer and gold leaf, paulownia, bamboo grass, and phoenix design.

35. Covered bowl, Hidehira lacquer.

36. Five nested bowls, *maki-e* lacquer, paulownia design.

37. Set of three covered Meigetsu type bowls, lacquer with shell inlay, cherry blossom pattern.

38. Bowls, red and black lacquer.

39. Rectangular teabowl, black Oribe ware, flower design.

40. Teabowl, Incised Karatsu ware.

41. Teabowls.
Clockwise from top left: Shino ware, Red Raku ware,
Oribe ware, Black Oribe ware, incised *mishima* ware.

TEA CUPS

42. Cylindrical tea cup, Mino ware, geometric pattern.   43. Tea cup by Kanjirō Kawai.

44. Three tea cups by Shōji Hamada.

RICE BOWLS

45. Rice bowl, Seto ware, dot pattern.

46. Rice bowl, Imari porcelain, fan design.

47. Rice bowl, Seto porcelain, willow tree design.

48. Rice bowl, Seto ware, net pattern.

49. Rice bowl, Seto ware, "wheatstraw" pattern.

SHALLOW DISHES, PLATES, AND PLATTERS

50. Modern dishes and plates. Clockwise from top left: Long, footed plate, cross-shaped dish, three plates, irregular plate, leaf-shaped plate, plate (center) all by Rosanjin Kitaōji; two dishes by Shōji Hamada.

51. Large dish, Karatsu ware, pine tree design.

52. Large dish, Karatsu ware, iris design.

53. Large dish, Kutani ware, lotus pond and kingfisher design.

54. Square dish, Kutani ware, rice field paths design.

89

55. Platter, Imari porcelain, depicting map of Japan and Pacific region.

56. Platter, Imari porcelain, depicting the Fifty-Three Stages of the Tōkaidō Highway.

57. Dish, Imari porcelain, resist rabbit design with spray glaze.

58. Dish, Kakiemon style porcelain, sleeve design.

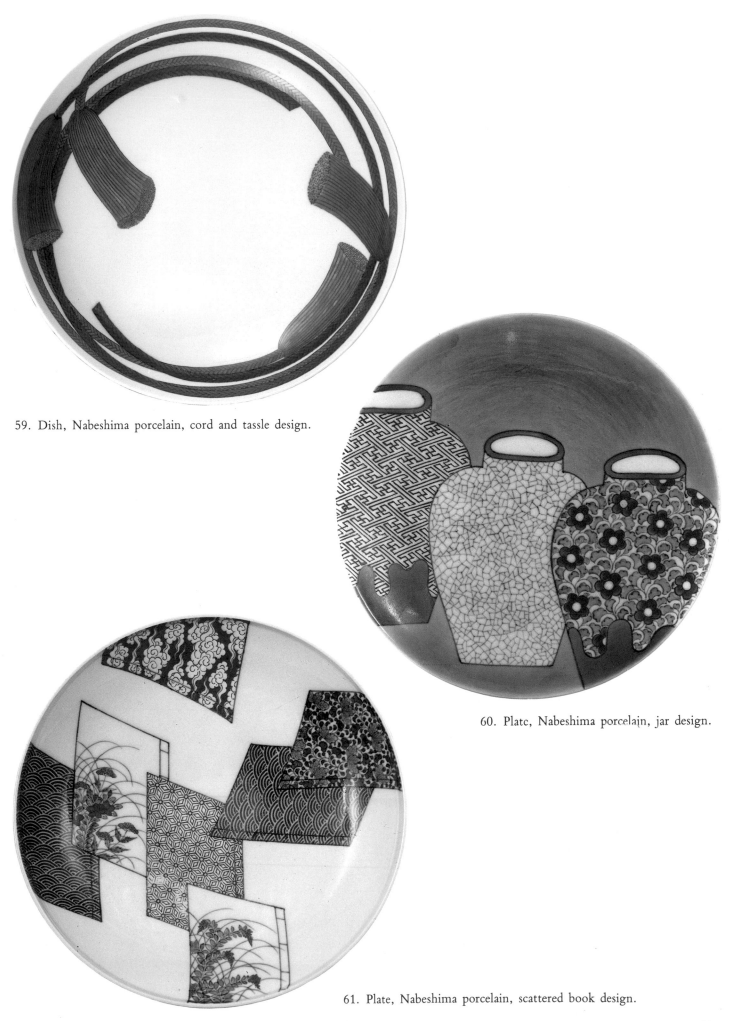

59. Dish, Nabeshima porcelain, cord and tassle design.

60. Plate, Nabeshima porcelain, jar design.

61. Plate, Nabeshima porcelain, scattered book design.

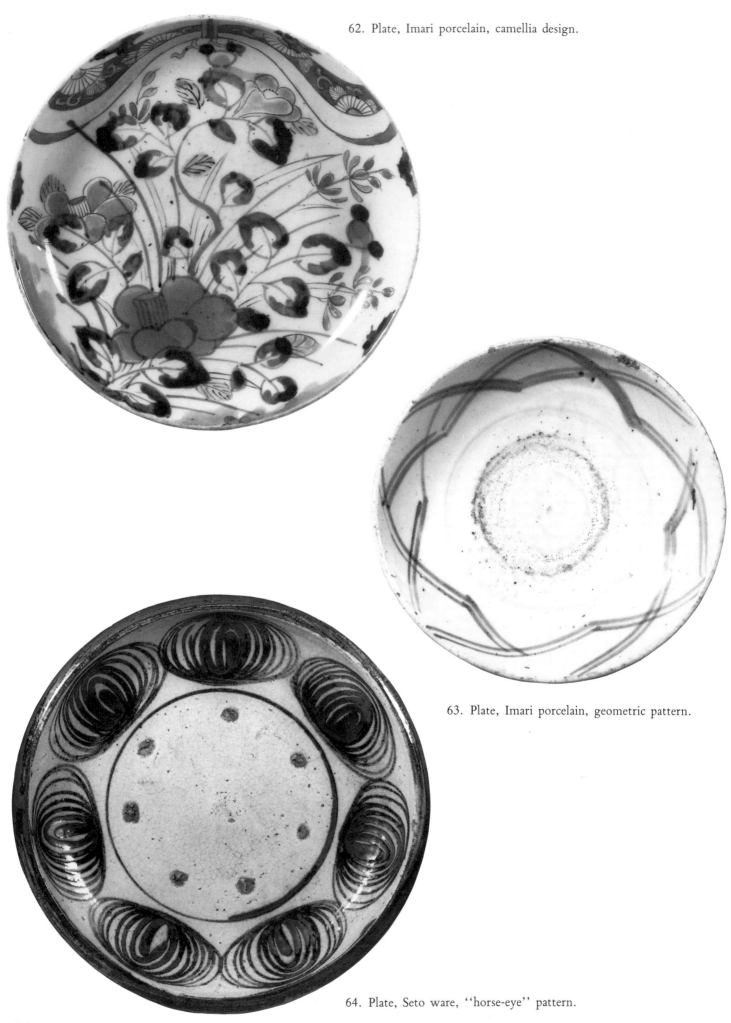

62. Plate, Imari porcelain, camellia design.

63. Plate, Imari porcelain, geometric pattern.

64. Plate, Seto ware, "horse-eye" pattern.

65. Plate, Seto ware, iris design.

66. Plate, Seto ware, landscape design.

67. Four square dishes (from a set of twelve) by Ogata Kenzan.
Clockwise from upper right:
February: pheasant and cherry blossoms
March: skylark and wisteria
December: calligraphy
June: wild pinks and cormorant

68. Square dish by Ogata Kenzan; Mt. Fuji design painted by Ogata Kōrin.

SERVING
BOWLS

69. Left, top to bottom:
Shallow bowls by Shōji
Hamada, Kanjirō Kawai,
and Shōji Hamada;
right: two bowls by Rosanjin
Kitaōji.

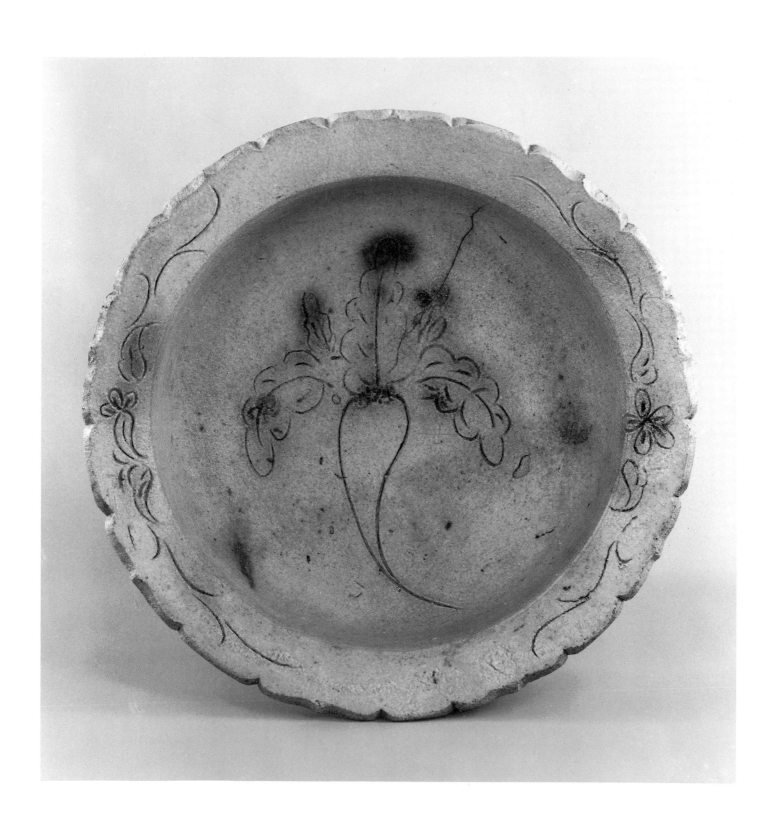

70. Large bowl, Kiseto ware, radish design.

71. Large bowl, Karatsu ware, flower and grass design; deep bowl, Karatsu ware, flower and grass design.

72. Shino and Oribe pieces
Clockwise from top right: Square bowl, Shino ware; shallow bowl, Gray
Shino ware; lidded box, Oribe ware; handled bowl, Oribe ware.

73. Shallow bowl, Green Kutani porcelain, *noshi* banner design.

74. Shallow bowls, Green Kutani porcelain,
flower and vine pattern; floating fan design.

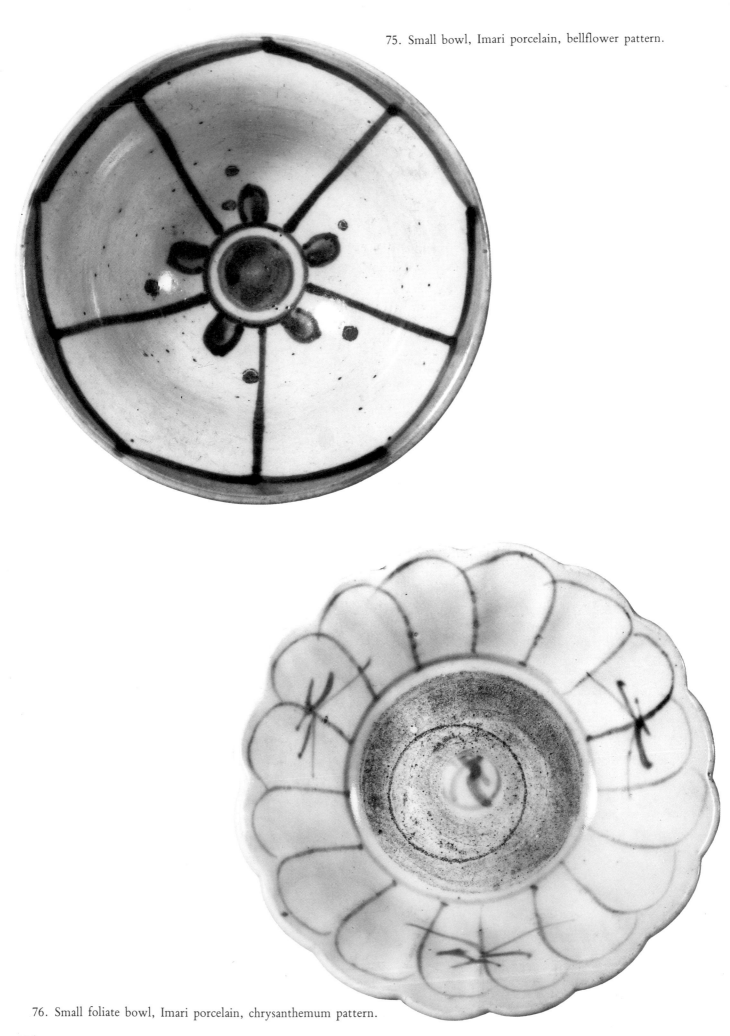

75. Small bowl, Imari porcelain, bellflower pattern.

76. Small foliate bowl, Imari porcelain, chrysanthemum pattern.

77. Large shallow bowl, Imari porcelain, landscape design.

MUKŌZUKE DISHES

78. Modern *mukōzuke* dishes.

79. Hexagonal deep *mukōzuke*.

80. Hexagonal deep *mukōzuke*.

81. Footed deep *mukōzuke*.

82. Fan-shaped *mukōzuke*.

83. Crescent-shaped *mukōzuke*.

84. Rhomboid *mukōzuke*.

85. Plover-shaped *mukōzuke*.

86. Depressed-rim *mukōzuke*.

87. Boat-shaped *mukōzuke*.

88. "Sand billow" *mukōzuke*.

89. Foliate *mukōzuke* dish, monochrome
Oribe ware, mule and rider design.

90. Foliate *mukōzuke* dish, monochrome
Oribe ware, heron design.

91. *Mukōzuke* dishes, Kiseto ware,
flower and grass designs.

113

92. Cylindrical *mukōzuke* dish, Shino ware, willow design.

93. Persimmon flower-shaped *mukōzuke* dishes, Karatsu ware.

94. Camellia-shaped *mukōzuke* dishes, camellia pattern, by Ogata Kenzan.

95. *Mukōzuke* dishes, Karatsu ware style, by Ogata Kenzan.

96. Set of *mukōzuke* dishes, maple leaves in the
Tatsuta River design, by Ogata Kenzan.

PICNIC BOX SET

97. Lacquered picnic box set (with pewter saké bottles), *maki-e* lacquer, scenes from the Yoshiwara pleasure quarter.

118

TIERED FOOD BOXES

98. Tiered food box, *maki-e* lacquer, *noshi* banner design.

99. Tiered food box, *maki-e* lacquer, umbrella design.

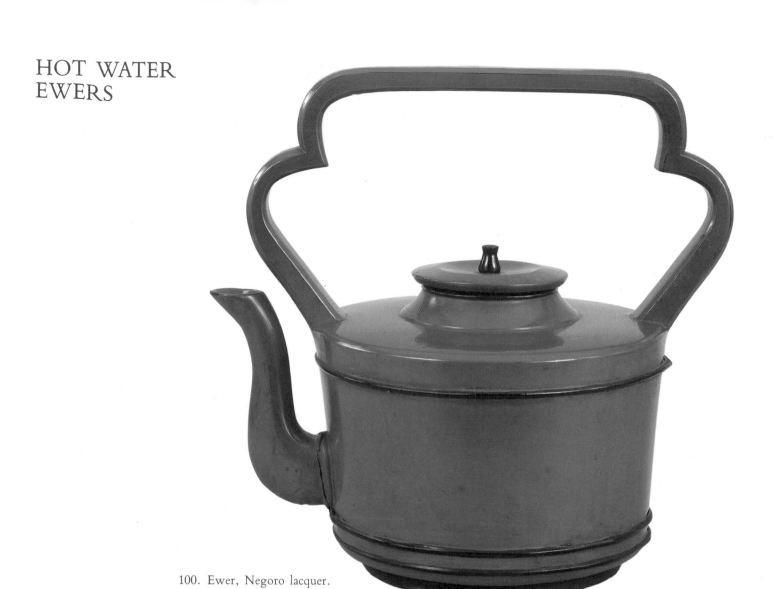

100. Ewer, Negoro lacquer.

101. Hot water ewer, lacquer.

SAKÉ SERVERS

102. Saké server, Negoro lacquer.

103. Saké server, Shino-Oribe ware.

104. Gourd-shaped saké server, Kakiemon style porcelain, grapevine, bird, and cord design.

105. Saké server, Nagasaki glass.

106. Geometric saké server, Satsuma ware.

107. Contemporary teapots and cups
Clockwise from top right: Teapot, Onta ware; teapot, Shussai ware; tea cup
by Jirō Kinjō; three Oribe and Shino style tea cups; tea cup, Mashiko ware.

SAKÉ BOTTLES AND CUPS

108. Modern saké bottles and cups
Far left, front to back: Saké cup, Bizen ware, by Tōyō Kanashige; Hagi ware, by Kyūsetsu Miwa; Bizen ware, by Yū Fujiwara. On tray, clockwise from back left: Saké cup, hatch and dot pattern; two saké bottles on ends by Rosanjin Kitaōji, two in center Shōji Hamada; saké cups, Red Shino ware style by Rosanjin Kitaōji, Hagi ware by Shimbei Sakakura XIV, engobe by Masaya Yoshimura, (center) porcelain footed cup. Tray, red lacquer, by Tōru Matsuzaki.

SAKÉ BOTTLES

109. Boat saké bottle, Tamba ware.

110. Candle-shaped saké bottle, Tamba ware.

111. Saké bottle, Bizen ware.

112. Purse-shaped saké bottle, Tamba ware.

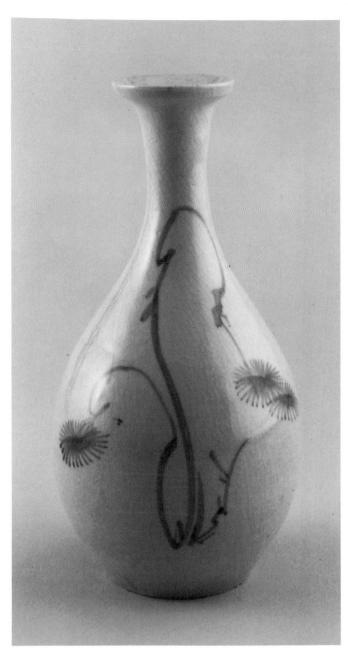

113. Saké bottle, Imari porcelain, pine design.

114. Gourd-shaped saké bottle, Shino-Oribe ware, grapevine design.

115. Twisted gourd-shaped saké bottle, Kutani porcelain, flower and grass design.

116. Twisted gourd-shaped saké bottle, Imari porcelain.

117. Sauce server, spring grasses design, by Ogata Kenzan.

118. Sauce servers by Rosanjin Kitaōji.

TRAY-TABLES

119. *Takatsuki* type tray-table, Negoro lacquer.

120. *Tsuigasane* type tray-table, Negoro lacquer.

121. *Kakeban* type tray-table, Negoro lacquer.

122. Butterfly-leg type tray-table and bowls, *maki-e* lacquer, paulownia design.

123. Tray, polychrome lacquer.

124. Box table, green and red lacquer.

NOODLE-SAUCE CUPS

125. Noodle-sauce cups, porcelain.

CHOPSTICK RESTS

126. Chopstick rests, vegetable shapes; *Rikyū-bashi* chopsticks,
chopstick rest, by Rosanjin Kitaōji.

IV

FOODS AND UTENSILS IN JAPANESE HISTORY

PREHISTORIC TIMES

JŌMON AND YAYOI PERIODS

Origins of Japanese Tableware

Jōmon culture, which lasted some eight millennia (ca. 8,000 B.C. to ca. 200 B.C.), stands out among primitive cultures of the world for the vast number of clay pots that it produced. The name *Jōmon*, meaning a rope or cord mark, is taken from elaborate ropelike markings on the surface of the pottery.

Studies of shell mounds and peat strata have brought to light various details of the eating habits of the Jōmon inhabitants of Japan. Seafood was abundant—some three hundred kinds of clams and other shellfish have been identified. Nuts, chiefly walnuts, horse chestnuts, chestnuts, and several varieties of acorn, were broken open and eaten straight from the shell or ground in stone mortars or metates with stone pestles and cooked in earthenware vessels.

The first known eating pots in Japan are earthenware vessels fashioned by coiling a rope of clay. The earliest examples are round bottomed, but later they were made with pointed bottoms (Pl. 128); this pointed bottom was stuck in the ground and a cooking fire was kindled around the portion above ground.

As culinary methods increased in sophistication, corresponding changes appeared in vessels as well. Clay pots with spouts (Pl. 129) have been found, along with deep bowls, jars, shallow bowls, and plates. Jōmon plates are rare, however, this being one of the last shapes to appear.

The Yayoi period lasted several hundred years, from about 250 B.C. to about A.D. 250. (The name is taken from a shell mound discovered in Yayoi-cho, Tokyo, in 1884.) In mid-Yayoi, around the beginning of the Christian era, a landmark event occurred: rice, native to Southeast Asia, was brought to Japan, and eating habits and ways of life were slowly transformed. Henceforth there

127. "April," detail of eight-fold screen, *Tsukinami fūzoku* ("Seasonal Customs and Monthly Amusements").

129. Spouted pot, late Jōmon period.

128. Pot with pointed bottom, middle Jōmon period.

130. Small bowl, Yayoi period.

131. Large jar, Yayoi period.

was a steady transition from hunting and gathering to agriculture, with a parallel increase in settled habitation.

With the introduction of metallurgy from the continent during the Yayoi period, the development of metal blade tools allowed the fashioning of wooden eating utensils. Digs at Yayoi sites have yielded wooden buckets, dishes, tables, bowls, spoons, chopsticks, and the like. The relative lack of diversity in Yayoi pottery, compared to that of the Jōmon period, is believed to result from the extensive use of such wooden utensils.

While in Jōmon pottery the most common shapes are deep and shallow bowls, the prevailing shapes in Yayoi pottery are jars for storage and urns for cooking. Pots for boiling food are also common to both periods. Large jars such as in Plate 131 had little decoration and were probably used to store seed rice.

132. Canteen-shaped flask (*teibei*), Sué ware.

133. Barrel-shaped flask (*yokobei*), Sué ware.

ANCIENT TIMES

TUMULUS, ASUKA, AND HAKUHŌ PERIODS

From Earthenware to Stoneware: The Advent of Sué Pottery

The dietary habits of the Japanese from the fourth century (when a unified nation arose with its center in what is now the Nara/Kyoto/Osaka area) through the seventh century (when great changes were brought on by the influence of China) bear scrutiny.

Early sources such as the *Kojiki* (*Records of Ancient Matters*; 712), *Nihon shoki* (*Chronicles of Japan*; 720) and *fudoki* (ancient gazetteers) mention a wide variety of utensils and offer evidence that staple foods were mainly millet, brown rice, barley, and legumes.

Rice was prepared by steaming in an earthenware vessel called a *koshiki*. Steamed rice (*ii*) and other grains became staples starting around the fifth century, marking a major change in food culture. Vegetables and game (such as boar, duck, and snipe) furnished additional nutrition.

This age was dominated by the imperial court at Yamato. Huge tombs were built, giving the name to this Tumulus period (250–552). Excavations in some of these tumuli have brought to light a wide range of cooking and serving utensils.

Two main types of pottery appeared. One, a brown, unglazed, and low-fired ware called *haji*, is a derivation of Yayoi pottery. *Haji* ware was formed by coiling and paddling and is relatively thin walled. Made by professional artisans in each community, *haji* ware was used for everyday utensils as well as for ceremonial and funerary purposes. *Haji* ware urns, large jars, footed vessels, bowls, and plates are among those excavated.

Sué, the other representative type of ancient pottery, was made by a new technique introduced from the kingdom of Paekche in southern Korea. It was soon produced throughout Japan, fired in a reducing atmosphere in special kilns built half or wholly below ground, at temperatures of at least 1000° C. Gray in color, vitreous and occasionally showing natural ash glaze, *sué* ware was well suited for tableware. It was also resistant to humid-ity, which made it convenient for storing grain. Unlike *haji* ware, it was made on a potter's wheel. Many beautiful pieces survive.

Common types of *sué* pottery include footed and pedestalled vessels, large and small plates, bowls, large jars, and ewers. Specialized containers include globular flat-bottomed flasks (known as *heibei*); flat-bottomed canteen-shaped flasks (called *teibei*; Pl. 132); *yokobei* (Pl. 133), made by joining two deep dishes and attaching a neck on top; *kangata-hei*, small flasks with extra tall necks and wide lips; and *hazō*, doughnut-shaped flasks with holes from which saké or other beverages could be sipped through bamboo straws.

NARA PERIOD

Growing Chinese Influence; Shōsō-in Treasures

From 710 to 784, Japan's capital was at Heijō-kyō, corresponding roughly to the present city of Nara. The capital was closely modeled on the Chinese Tang dynasty capital of Chang-an. Political and administrative systems also emulated the Chinese model. In this way a strong, unified sovereign state came into being.

Among the provisions of the Yōrō code (718), one of the earliest statements of Japanese law based on Chinese models, was the compulsory service code, stipulating various articles of food to be contributed by each province. The main categories of foods mentioned are fish, shellfish, seaweed, grains, and seasonings such as salt, *hishio* (an ancestor of soy sauce), vinegar, and oil.

In recent years a vast assortment of wooden markers has been unearthed from the site of the former Heijō Palace, inscribed with contemporary names for various foods. These findings constitute direct evidence that foods were indeed transported from all over the country to the capital. These were primarily preserved foods, largely dried or salted. The development of various methods of preserving food meant that provisions could be carried to the capital year round to ensure the Nara court a stable and varied food supply.

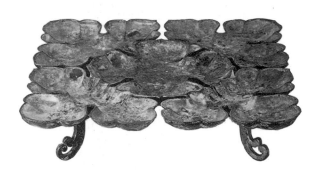

134. Bowl, three-colored glaze.　　　135. Carafe, clear glass.　　　136. Foliate dish, lacquer on wood.

Another noteworthy development was the institution of court banquets and other annual events at which formal meals were served. The emperor's meals, known as *kugo*, were artistically arranged with specially chosen utensils. Clearly the emphasis was less on flavor than on an artful appearance—an early sign of this enduring feature of Japanese haute cuisine.

A popular food in the Nara period, as indicated by food lists in the compulsory service code, was seaweed. Large quantities of sun-dried *wakame* were transported to the capital. A by-product of the sun-drying process was glutamic acid, which serves to enhance flavors; today it is a widely used flavor-enhancing agent in Japanese cooking.

Also during this period, a method for making rudimentary soy sauce was introduced from China and Korea, and a special Soy Sauce Bureau was established in the Department of the Imperial Household. This early form of soy sauce, *hishio*, was prized not only for its flavor but also as a food preservative, due to enzymes formed in the process of fermentation.

Tableware of the Nara period is well represented by the superb collection in the Shōsō-in repository. Many of these items traveled to Japan over the Silk Road, becoming prized possessions of Emperor Shōmu (r. 724–49). Generally, vessels were put to different uses according to their materials: silver bowls, for example, were used for rice, wooden ones for broth, and earthenware ones for water. Particularly noteworthy are three-color glazed ceramic dishes (Pl. 134) modeled after those made in Tang China. (Widespread use of applied glazes did not occur in Japan until the early seventeenth century.)

Metal table utensils in Shōsō-in include six- and twelve-lobed oblong cups made of gilded bronze, a foliate cup made of silver, nested bowls made of an alloy of copper, tin, and lead, and a variety of silver bowls, jars, and water pitchers. Glass drinking implements include a dark blue glass goblet, a white glass carafe (Pl. 135), a green glass twelve-lobed oblong cup, and various bowls. A number

of wooden implements also survive, among them flower-shaped dishes of lacquered wood with colored motifs, such as the one in Plate 136; a tray with painted motifs in oil colors; a high-footed vessel, perhaps used for sweets; an assortment of lacquered bowls; and a Persian ewer made of bamboo basketwork, covered with cloth and lacquered.

HEIAN PERIOD
Toward a Synthesis of Chinese and Native Styles
From 794 to 1185 the capital was at Heian-kyō, on the site of modern Kyoto. Heian culture, which flourished among courtiers and aristocrats, continued to be strongly influenced by the Chinese mainland, and, in food as in all else, Chinese techniques and amenities were readily absorbed. This was also a crucial age of transition, as imported culinary styles were naturalized and mixed with indigenous styles of the Nara period and before to produce a distinctively Japanese cuisine.

The *Ruijūzōyō-shō* ("Compendium of Miscellaneous Affairs"), a scroll painting depicting various Heian court practices and usages, shows a courtiers' meal with foods heaped on round, high-footed vessels (Pl. 137). The same scroll also depicts a grand feast held in 1116 on the 23rd day of the 1st month by Minister of the Interior Fujiwara no Tadamichi (1097–1164).

At such a repast, each court noble would be seated before an array of foods like those seen in Plate 138; the guest of honor, meanwhile, would be served dishes like those in Plate 139. Despite their festive appearance, meals were mainly prepared from dried foods, with very little fresh fruit or vegetables. Numerous seasonings and accompaniments are pictured: salt, vinegar, saké, *hishio*, dried and fresh fish, fruits and nuts, pastries fried in sesame oil. It is apparent, however, that the main focus was on creating an attractive display, not on subtleties of flavor or nutrition.

Guests sat before low rectangular tables called *daiban*, the largest of which measured some 240 centimeters across. Table utensils were all of silver, with soups and beverages

仁和寺嚴競馬行幸御膳并御遊酒肴事
保延二年九月廿八日

137.–140. From *Ruijūzōyō-shō* ("Compendium of Miscellaneous Affairs").
137. Courtier's meal on round, pedestalled tray-table.

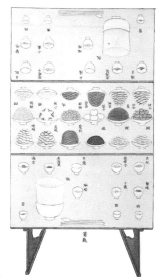

138. Court meal.

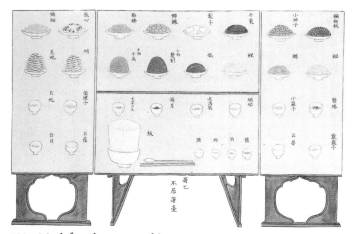

139. Meal for the guest of honor.

140. *Tonjiki* (midday snack).

served in special curved bowls and dry foods arranged in small flat dishes. Hard-textured steamed rice (*kowa-ii*) was heaped high and eaten with a silver spoon. Chopsticks and spoons were provided on a four-footed tray called, from its distinctive oblong shape, "horse's head tray" (*batō-ban*). The influence of Chinese manners may be seen in the large, shared table and in the use of spoons—both significant departures from native custom.

Detailed diagrams of Heian table utensils are to be found in *Chūjiruiki* ("Kitchen Miscellanea"), dated some time after 1295.

Meals were eaten twice daily, between 10:00 and 12:00 A.M. and again around 4:00 P.M. Lower-grade officials, however, also had a midday snack called *tonjiki*, consisting of oval rice cakes (Pl. 140). This gradually developed into a more substantial meal comparable to today's lunch.

Rice was prepared in several different ways. In addition to *kowa-ii*, eaten by the nobility, variations include: *hime-ii* (soft, boiled rice resembling that of today), *kayu* (gruel), and *abura-ii* (rice mixed with hempseed oil), among others.

At banquets, supplementary foods were often placed in a ring of dishes and bowls on a small table, with rice heaped high in the center. This special table setting, called *ōban*, was used when entertaining guests. Examples are found in the *Bandainagon ekotoba* (Pl. 144) and other Heian scroll paintings.

Drinking parties were also popular among the Heian nobility. *Gakizōshi emaki* ("Scrolls of Hungry Demons") contains a scene depicting such a party (Pl. 145). Several kinds of saké were served: a sweet variety called *kosaké*, an unrefined variety called *moromi*, and a fine-quality thick wine called *junshu*. Saké was often stored in decorated urns like the one in Plate 141.

Types of Heian serving tables (besides the *ōban*) include the *kakeban*, a graceful lacquered table with four curved legs set in a frame; *tsuigasane*, a plain wood tray set on a base with decorative holes cut in three or four sides; and *takatsuki*, a pedestalled lacquered table. Also used were

141. Urn, *maki-e* lacquer, bamboo, paulownia, and phoenix design.

142. Dishes, ash glaze.

143. Bowls, plates, and ewer, green glaze.

square serving trays (*oshiki*). *Yamai no sōshi* ("Diseases Scroll") shows *oshiki* being used at a typical commoners' meal (Pl. 146).

Heian eating utensils were extremely varied, being made from nearly every kind of material in use today. In the early Heian, ash-glazed pottery, covered by hand with ash and then fired at high temperatures, came into use (Pl. 142). Around the same time, green-glazed ceramics (Pl. 143) became popular for water pitchers, high-footed bowls, and plates—all common Chinese ceramic types. Lacquer ware was also prominent; large- and medium-sized red lacquered bowls (with or without lids) called *mari* were used for rice and gruel as well as water, saké, and cooked food. Stoneware dishes included a fairly small, shallow dish called *tsuki* or *kawarake*, used widely to hold water, saké, vinegar, *hishio*, and other liquids.

MEDIEVAL TIMES

KAMAKURA PERIOD

Fine Lacquer Ware, Zen Vegetarian Cuisine

During the Kamakura period (1185–1333), Japan was under the control not of courtiers and aristocrats, but of military men. The seat of government shifted east, from Kyoto to distant Kamakura. The vigorous military spirit of the age brought dynamic change, along with the growing influence of Zen sects. In the nation's culinary habits, three distinct currents emerged, associated respectively with the military, the aristocracy, and the Zen Buddhist clergy.

The kind of meal eaten by samurai of the time is suggested in a late Kamakura scroll painting entitled *Gosannen gassen emaki* ("The Three Years' War") (Pl. 147). A row of armor-clad men is seated on the floor, each facing his own table. In the center of each table is a bowl heaped high with rice, and surrounding it are three or four small dishes, each containing a different accompaniment. Each place setting also has a saké cup at one side. As this scene shows, meals were extremely simple, with a substantial portion of rice the main attraction.

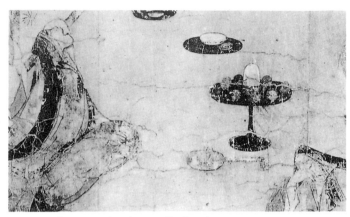

144. *Bandainagon ekotoba* scroll (detail).

145. *Gakizōshi emaki* ("Scrolls of Hungry Demons"; detail).

146. *Yamai no sōshi* ("Diseases scroll"; detail).

147. *Gosannen gassen emaki* scroll ("The Three Years' War"; detail).

148. *Kasuga gongen kenki emaki* scroll ("Miracles of the Shinto Deities of Kasuga"; detail).

Meals eaten by courtiers of this era are depicted in a series of twenty scrolls called the *Kasuga gongen kenki emaki* ("Miracles of the Shinto Deities of Kasuga"), painted in 1309 (Pl. 148). On a *kakeban* are a generous serving of rice, a bowl of soup, and two side dishes. Contemporary sources reveal that among the foods eaten were sea squirt, steamed abalone, fried octopus, *suwayari* (thin slices of dried, salted fish), salt, vinegar, and assorted fruit. Heian period precedent, as matters of layout and etiquette became increasingly formalized, continued to determine how, as well as what, courtiers ate.

The Buddhist vegetarian cuisine known as *shōjin ryōri* spread along with the rise of Zen Buddhism, gradually developing in sophistication until the mid-fourteenth century, when with the addition of *tōfu* and *konnyaku*, it reached its present form. In a Kamakura scroll entitled *Boki-ekotoba* ("The Life of Priest Kakunyo") (Pl. 149), vegetarian foods are seen being prepared in a temple kitchen filled with assorted utensils, including *magemono* (bentwood vessels), ceramic mortars, wooden ladles, bamboo baskets, and long-handled scoops. Stacked on shelves in the background are various serving tables and bowls.

In the Kamakura period, common people for the most part ate the same hard steamed brown rice that their ancestors had eaten. In temples, however, softer boiled rice and gruel were standard, and as the influence of the Zen sect expanded, gradually boiled rice became widely accepted.

Condiments of this period included fish broth, saké, salt, vinegar, *hishio*, and sweeteners like honey and dried powdered fruit. Each was served in a small dish, and diners dipped foods in these condiments.

Tea (whisked, not brewed) first became popular in the Kamakura period. The custom of tea drinking went on to become firmly established in the fourteenth and fifteenth centuries, laying the foundation for the later development of the tea ceremony. Early tea gatherings were quite informal; a variation on saké-drinking parties, they featured a merry game in which contestants took turns tasting different kinds of tea and guessing their place of origin.

Ceramics and lacquer ware are prominent among the tableware of the Kamakura period. By the mid-thirteenth century, different ceramic types were being made at Seto, influenced by Chinese Song dynasty celadon and white porcelain (Pl. 150). Other centers of ceramic production were Tokoname, Echizen, Suzu, and Bizen, where everyday items, principally tableware, were manufactured in large amounts.

Lacquer ware, though still beyond the reach of common people, was now used on formal occasions by both court nobles and the military class. Even Zen priests, used red lacquered dishes. Among the oldest surviving pieces of lacquer ware whose dates of manufacture are known are a bucket-shaped serving dish (Pl. 151) and serving trays, both square and round.

From around this time, itinerant woodworkers known as *kijishi* began peddling smooth wooden implements made on lathes or with blade tools. Bentwood work (*magemono*), made by softening a thin piece of wood in hot water and shaping it into a round container, was increasingly used.

Bamboo utensils also began to appear. No part of the plant went to waste: nodes, branches, and roots were each fashioned skillfully into a variety of baskets, scoops, and other utensils.

MUROMACHI PERIOD
The Emergence of Professional Cooks and Honzen Ryōri

In contrast to the simplicity that characterized the preceding age, the Muromachi period (1333–1568) was a time of rich cultural flowering, typified architecturally in structures like the Golden and Silver pavilions in Kyoto. Court and military traditions were united, continental contacts were revived, and Zen influence continued to grow. In the area of food, professional chefs contrived elaborate dishes, and the foundations of today's Japanese cuisine were laid.

Among the scroll paintings of the Muromachi period is a light, anonymous work known as *Shuhanron ekotoba*

149. *Boki ekotoba* scroll ("The Life of Priest Kakunyo"; detail).

150. Jar, Old Seto ware, stamped pattern of plum blossoms.

151. Bucket-shaped serving dish, Negoro lacquer.

("Debate over Food and Wine"), in which a drunkard, a teetotaler, and a moderate drinker expound in turn on their respective philosophies. Scattered throughout are representations of contemporary eating and drinking mores. Plate 152 shows a meal in a samurai household, Plate 153 a kitchen where cooks squat before huge chopping boards preparing fish and fowl, using special chopsticks called *manabashi*. At the hearth in the foreground various pots are boiling away. One man takes a taste, using a ladle made of a shell attached to a long wooden handle, while another takes the lid off another pot to check the contents.

Professional cooks known as *hōchōshi* ("kitchen-knife masters") appeared, and various schools of court cuisine emerged, each with its recommended ways of cutting fowl or fish. The structure of formal meals became standardized, consisting of the *honzen* (principal meal) followed by *ni no zen* and *san no zen* (second and third meals). Various rules governed the placement of cups and dishes on trays, as well as the kinds and combinations of foods served. This style of multicourse meal (*honzen ryōri*), still served on formal occasions, differs significantly from its modern Western counterpart; the Japanese way is not to present dishes singly but in groups, using a variety of containers and seeking to create, through the careful selection and arrangement of foods and utensils, an ambience of festivity and beauty.

A cookbook of the Shijō school published in 1489 contains the following instructions in its section on *kaishiki*, the practice of garnishing food with leaves or small leafy twigs: "Use leaves of white cedar, or *nandin* bamboo. Green maple leaves are unlucky. For auspicious occasions, the leaf should be right side up, for solemn ones, face down." Such techniques were an important means of heightening the visual appeal of food in an age lacking tableware of gay colors and striking patterns.

A major factor in the development of professional cooks was the Japanese custom of eating with chopsticks, which required that all foods be served in manageable, bite-sized

152, 153. *Shuhanron ekotoba* scroll ("Debate over Food and Wine"; details).

143

154. Rice container, Negoro lacquer.

155. Hexagonal bowl with legs, Negoro lacquer.

pieces. The test of a cook lay in how skillfully he could wield his knife and in how artfully he could arrange dishes composed of such bite-sized tidbits.

One classic dish that owes its development largely to the skills of the carving-knife masters is *sashimi*. It first added its freshness and pleasing variety of tastes, textures, and colors during the Muromachi period.

Soy sauce (*shōyu*) became popular in the mid-sixteenth century, at the end of this era. It was refined from the liquid of the fermented, salted grain mash known as *hishio*. As its use spread, soy sauce gradually became the paramount seasoning in Japan, contributing greatly to the development of the distinctive flavors of Japanese foods.

Another important development in the Muromachi period was the growing influence of the tea ceremony. In place of the games once played, now guests assembled quietly to savor tea and admire the simple beauty of tea utensils. Light meals known as *kaiseki ryōri* were served before the ceremonial tea. The novelty of this cuisine lay in its method of preparation: for the first time, seasonings were used during the cooking process. Before, cooked foods had been served cold and unseasoned, alongside various condiments; beginning with *kaiseki ryōri*, however, it became customary to serve warm foods with the flavors cooked in.

Of the extant Muromachi table utensils, certainly among the most attractive are the red lacquered pieces made by the priests of Negoro-dera, a temple in present Wakayama Prefecture. Used by priests and worshipers alike, Negoro lacquer had a modesty and simplicity of great freshness and appeal. Over the centuries, the vermilion has worn away, allowing the black lacquer beneath to show through for an effect of still greater beauty. A wide variety of Negoro utensils survive, including bucket-shaped serving dishes, rice-containers (Pl. 154), ewers, bowls, serving bowls (Pl. 155), saké bottles, and assorted serving tables and trays.

Muromachi ceramics were made at Seto, Tokoname, Shigaraki, Tamba, Bizen, Echizen, and other localities.

Mainly large jars and pots for agricultural use were produced.

MOMOYAMA PERIOD
Tea-Ceremony Cuisine and the Golden Age of Ceramics

The Momoyama period lasted less than fifty years, from the late sixteenth century to the early seventeenth; yet it was a crucial time in Japanese political and cultural history. The process of national unification begun by Oda Nobunaga (1534–82) was carried on by Toyotomi Hideyoshi (1536–98), bringing the country closer to a strong one-man rule. At the same time, contacts with Western civilization were deepened, and a burst of youthful energies brought about a new cultural flowering.

In the nation's diet, Western cooking (known then as *namban ryōri*, "southern barbarian cooking") was introduced, along with new foods such as corn, watermelon, sweet potatoes, and tomatoes. Among Christian daimyos the eating of beef became popular; Plate 158 shows a freshly unloaded cargo of smoked meat. The Western custom of deep-frying foods (*namban-yaki*) also gained acceptance. Tempura, now a classic Japanese dish, is said to derive from a certain fried fish dish eaten by Portuguese Christians at Friday observances called *témporas*.

Chinese dishes were also popular during this period. At first the rich flavors from their many oils and spices were pleasantly exotic, but in time the taste was modified to suit the lighter Japanese palate. These Japanized dishes, known as *shippoku ryōri* ("tabletop cooking"), were extremely popular. No doubt the unaccustomed practice of sitting grouped around one large table, with everyone helping himself from one array of dishes, added to the pleasure.

Polished rice, refined sakés, and sugar made their debuts in the Momoyama period, and soy sauce became the dominant seasoning. *Wasabi* horseradish and stocks made of kelp and dried bonito came into use as well, setting the trend toward the modern form of Japanese cooking.

A wide variety of fish and seafood was consumed, including carp, sea bream, pike, conger, sea bass, abalone,

156. From *Shokunin zukushi-e* ("Catalogue of Crafts-men")—The Bentwood (*magemono*) Craftsmen.

157. *Rakuchū Rakugai* screen ("Sights In and Around the Capital"; detail).

158. *Namban* screen ("Southern Barbarian"; detail).

159. Hexagonal tiered food box, gold lacquer with shell inlay.

160. Spice container set (small porcelain jars covered with *maki-e* lacquer with floral motifs.

161. Teabowl, black Raku ware, by Chōjirō.

jellyfish, shrimp, flounder, herring roe, octopus, squid, cod, and eel. Popular varieties of fowl were crane, snipe, swan, and skylark. Processed foodstuffs like *karasumi* (dried mullet roe) and *kamaboko* (fish paste) were also popular. Methods of preparation were varied: a Momoyama gourmet might enjoy his fish as *sashimi* (thinly sliced, raw), *sushi* (raw with vinegared rice), *yakimono* (roasted), *aburimono* (grilled), *irimono* (parched, or fried in oil), *shirumono* (soup), or *aemono* (chopped and dressed with sauce).

Characterized by a proliferation of new foods and styles of cooking and eating, the period showed a strong tendency toward luxury and extravagance. Banquets given by men of power were remarkable for their splendor. When Emperor Goyōzei (r. 1586–1611) visited Toyotomi Hideyoshi in 1588 at his sumptuous palace, according to the *Gyōkō okondate-ki* ("Record of Menus for Imperial Visits") as many as nine different dishes of fish and fowl were served; tables were spread with dazzling utensils of gold and silver on sheets of paper decorated with gold.

Representative of Momoyama food utensils are the showy *maki-e* (lacquer with gold and silver embellishment) dishes at Kōdai-ji in Kyoto. This temple, where Hideyoshi's widow retired after her husband's death, owns numerous *maki-e* tables, bowls, trays, and other articles used during their marriage. In particular, a *Kakeban* type tray-table and a set of spice containers with designs of autumn flowers and grasses (Pl. 160) exemplify the sumptuous taste of this era.

At the same time, through the tea cult there arose an opposing trend of equal and lasting significance. As demand grew for articles used in the tea ceremony, the aesthetics of *wabi* and *sabi*—advocating simple, austere beauty—deepened in meaning and influence. Utensils chosen or ordered made by tea masters such as the great Sen no Rikyū (1522–91) were highly original, exemplifying an unconventional standard of beauty that has continued to resonate in Japanese culture ever since. A teabowl favored by Rikyū, shown in Plate 161, has a stark con-

figuration that was then completely new; in time such shapes became stylized and were copied in kilns around the country.

On the 12th day of the 1st month in 1587, Sen no Rikyū hosted a representative tea ceremony for a Kyushu merchant named Kamiya Sōtan. Records indicate that they ate only from dishes of black or vermilion lacquer on lacquered trays. Among the serving vessels used were medium-sized bowls, flared soupbowls, basins, nested boxes, shallow bowls of plain wood on the outside and black lacquer on the inside, cake trays, and *fuchidaka* (square trays with high raised edges). The menu was also simple and light (featuring burdock boiled in soy sauce, chicken soup, and pickles), in line with Rikyū's dictum that "a meal should be enough to ward off hunger, a house enough to keep off the rain."

Rikyū's Zen-based philosophy of *wabi*, which might be called the aesthetics of restraint, was a strong force for moderation in an age when formal meals often were the ultimate in extravagance. *Kaiseki ryōri* had a profound influence on the long-term development of Japanese cuisine, imparting to it a new spiritual dimension.

Ceramic styles also underwent unprecedented change and rejuvenation; indeed the Momoyama period is often called the golden age of Japanese ceramics. As the center of production shifted from Seto to Mino, Seto artisans gathered in Mino under the aegis of the powerful Toki clan and set up numerous kilns, producing Shino, Kiseto, Oribe, and other wares of a vigor, diversity, and exuberance unmatched in previous ages and since. In particular, the dishes and bowls commissioned and inspired by the tea master Furuta Oribe (1544–1615) show a brilliant novelty of design that reflects the influence of Western civilization (Pls. 79–88).

EDO PERIOD
The Rise of Restaurants and the Crystallization of Japanese Cuisine

After the death of Hideyoshi, Tokugawa Ieyasu

162. "The Kawaguchi Pleasure District" screen (detail).

(1542–1616) consolidated the government's power, becoming shogun in 1603 and establishing his capital at Edo (present Tokyo). For over two and one-half centuries, Japan enjoyed peace under the isolationist policies of the Tokugawa shogunate, and Japanese culture entered a period of maturity in which the affluent urban merchant class played a central role.

In the first half of the Edo period a distinctive culinary culture developed in the Kyoto-Osaka area as part of this new urban culture. Osaka, known as "the nation's kitchen," boasted an unprecedented range of foods from which well-to-do townsmen could choose. *Kawaguchi yū-kaku-zu byōbu* ("The Kawaguchi Pleasure District"; Pl. 162), a screen portraying red-light districts in the Kyoto-Osaka area, suggests the vitality and epicureanism of Edo period commoners. Safer and swifter transport, along with the establishment of settled peace, allowed foodstuffs to be transported easily from all over the country in greater variety than ever before. As this screen painting shows, products were taken ashore from riverboats and cooked immediately in waterfront kitchens, then arranged in beautiful lacquered and ceramic vessels and carried off to waiting guests.

Meanwhile, the fast-growing city of Edo developed its own style of cuisine, dating from about the first quarter of the nineteenth century. Numerous cookbooks were published concerning preparation of such foods as soups; *aemono* (chopped fish and or vegetables in dressing); *nimono* (boiled food); *namono* (steamed vegetables); *hitashimono* (greens boiled then flavored with soy sauce); *yakimono* (pan-fried or grilled foods), including *tamago-yaki* (egg rolls); *agemono* (deep-fried foods); *sashimi; sushi*, both boxed and hand-rolled; and *tsukemono* (pickles). *Tōfu* was used in so many different ways that it was called the "food of one hundred flavors" (Pls. 163, 164).

Meanwhile, ceremonial meals of the Edo court and military aristocracy—wedding banquets and the like—continued to adhere to classical standards. At the same time, *kaiseki ryōri* became increasingly popular and was

163. Banquet scene, from *Shirōto bōchō* ("Cooking for Amateurs").

164. Sushi making, from *Shirōto bōchō* ("Cooking for Amateurs").

147

165. *Kaiseki* setting, from *Ryōri haya shinan*.

166. Chinese-style vegetarian meal, from *Fucha ryōri shō* ("A Selection of Vegetarian Food").

developed to its present form. Great importance was attached to the quality and flavor of individual foods and to harmony of food and vessel. A book entitled *Ryōri haya shinan*, published in 1822, shows a sample *kaiseki* setting of this time with a carefully arranged array of dishes and cups (Pl. 165).

Everyday fare was, of course, far simpler. For domestic servants, a typical day's menu might include, besides rice, only miso soup for breakfast, seaweed and fried tofu for lunch, and pickled vegetables for dinner. Fish was eaten rarely, perhaps once in ten days.

The origin of restaurants was documented by novelist Ihara Saikaku (1642–93) in *Saikaku okimiyage* ("Saikaku's Parting Present"), published in 1693. He writes of a popular teahouse inside the precincts of the Asakusa Kannon Shrine that served *chameshi* (rice boiled in tea with salt), tofu soup, beans boiled in soy, and other dishes under the collective name "Nara tea." As teahouses lavished increasing care on their menus, gradually they became popular places to eat. By 1725, several restaurants located side by side on the great rivers of Edo had direct connection with riverside fish markets and were renowned—among ordinary folk as well as wealthy townsmen—for the freshness of their food.

A century later, the picture was different: "A tall building every five steps, a stately mansion every ten—and all, to the last, are places of eating and drinking" (*Ichiwa ichigon*). Particularly celebrated were the Yaozen of Asakusa and the Hirasei of Fukagawa, which together boasted the finest food in town, prepared by master chefs. Around 1835, many famous establishments were immortalized in a series of woodblock prints by Hiroshige (1797–1858) entitled *Edo kōmei kaiteizukushi* ("Famous Restaurants of Edo") (Pls. 167, 168).

One such restaurant, the Bōdaran (or Masuya) in Fukagawa, was run by a man named Shukuami. In October 1781, he was invited to the home of Fuse, a master of satirical verse. The menu was the ultimate in lavishness,

offering clear evidence that Japanese cuisine had reached its highest level. Utensils for the occasion were blue-and-white Chinese porcelain, in keeping with the taste for things Chinese shared by literati. The following day, when Shukuami hosted a return banquet at the Bōdaran, he avoided Chinese porcelain, deliberately confining himself to Japanese wares. He also commented that while his friend's meal had been faultless in both preparation and serving, the many sublime flavors had led to a feeling of satiety. It was essential, he cautioned, that a meal should tire neither the palate nor the stomach; it was inexcusable to serve so much food that by the end of the meal one's guests could eat no more.

The perfection of Japanese culinary arts was accompanied by a growing consensus concerning which foods to serve in what vessels. Two centuries before, during Hideyoshi's Korean expeditions of 1592 and 1597, a number of daimyos had brought Korean potters back to Japan. These craftsmen set up kilns in the domains of these and other daimyos and began to produce porcelain in Kyushu. Porcelain became favored over other wares and in time all but replaced lacquer ware.

In the Edo period, pottery flourished in many regions of the country, and a range of distinctive and colorful ceramic traditions developed. Among the most celebrated wares are Takatori, Hirado, Agano, Hagi, Karatsu, and Kutani.

Both at home and abroad, demand was particularly high for Imari porcelain, produced in the Arita area but named for the port from which it was shipped. Imari porcelains display a wide range of shape, color, and design, seen in both blue-and-white porcelain and in colorful overglaze enameled wares (Pls. 169, 170). Enameled porcelains (Pl. 171) were exported from the mid-seventeenth century to Europe, where they had a great impact and inspired numerous copies.

Famous among the porcelains of northern Kyushu is Nabeshima ware, made exclusively for the Saga clan by

167. Yaozen restaurant, from the print series *Edo kōmei kaitei zukushi* ("Famous Restaurants of Edo"), by Hiroshige.

168. Aoyagi restaurant, from the print series *Edo kōmei kaitei zukushi* ("Famous Restaurants of Edo"), by Hiroshige.

169. Boat-shaped bowl, Kakiemon style porcelain.

170. Saké bottle, Imari porcelain.

171. Lidded bowl, Imari porcelain, flower carts and women design.

172. Teabowl, scale pattern, by Nonomura Ninsei.

173. Tea (*sencha*) set by Aoki Mokubei.

174. Tray with cut-corners, porcelain, flowers, birds, and fish design, by Okuda Eisen.

175. Large bowl, cherry blossoms and maple tree design, by Nin'ami Dōhachi.

clan artisans. Unavailable commercially, this ware was reserved for gift-giving by the clan lords and has a corresponding elegance and precision of design (Pls. 59–61).

Kyoto ware (*Kyō-yaki*) was begun early in the Edo period by a Kyoto potter named Nonomura Ninsei (active in the Kambun era, 1661–73). Sought after by court aristocracy and tea ceremony adepts as well, his works have classic beauty, and exerted some influence (Pl. 172). At the end of the seventeenth century, the master potter Ogata Kenzan (1663–1743) opened his own kiln. A pupil of Ninsei, he produced many works with landscape or floral patterns, both alone and with his elder brother, the famed painter Ogata Kōrin (Pl. 68).

By the nineteenth century, the number of kilns had greatly multiplied nationwide, and for the first time ordinary people began using ceramics for daily meals. Every Japanese-style utensil of today had, by this time, made its appearance, including large and small dishes, rice bowls, noodle bowls, cooking pots, pouring bowls, bottles, covered dishes and jars, and so on.

Both the affluent merchant class and the literati were able at this time to pursue lives of greater freedom, taking up new interests and pastimes. One result was that *sencha* (brewed tea) became popular among Kyoto literati and then spread around the country, increasing the demand for ceramic ware (Pl. 173).

Okuda Eisen (1753–1811) produced excellent Chinese-style porcelain in Kyoto (Pl. 174). He also trained many disciples, among them Aoki Mokubei (1767–1833), Nin'ami Dōhachi (1783–1855) (Pl. 175), and Eiraku Hozen (1795–1854).

The Edo period also saw a new material being used for tableware: glass. In the Momoyama period, glassware brought over by missionaries had been revered as a symbol of Western civilization.

In fact, the art of glass production was known in antiquity, but had been effectively lost in Japan. It was revived in the seventeenth century, first in Nagasaki, then

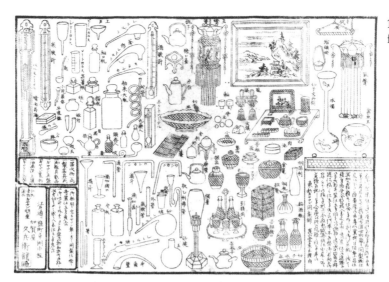

in Kyoto and Osaka, and by 1715 it was being made in Edo as well. A print by Utamaro (1753–1806) entitled *Biidoroshi* ("Glass-Blowers"), from the series *Fujin shokunin burui* ("Types of Female Craftsmen"), shows various hand-blown bottles and other articles (Pl. 177).

Glass articles sold in Edo from the Bunsei era to the Kaei era (1818–54) can be seen in an advertising circular for Kagaya, a contemporary store (Pl. 176). In this melange of Japanese, Chinese, and European things, several distinctively Japanese forms can be discerned. Among them are *kumijū* (tiered boxes), *jikirō* (round lidded containers), *choku* (saké cups), *tokkuri* (saké bottles), *mitsugumi sakazuki* (set of three large saké cups), and *chōshi* (saké servers).

MODERN TIMES

MEIJI, TAISHŌ, AND SHŌWA PERIODS
Coexistence of Japanese and Western Tableware

The Meiji Restoration of 1868 launched Japan on the path to modernization; the changes affected every facet of life, including what and how people ate.

Meat-eating had long been taboo in Japan; due to Buddhist influence, it was considered a source of defilement. In 1872 the ban on eating meat was lifted, and *gyūnikuya* ("beef houses") offering a beef dish soon were doing brisk business. The dish was called *gyūnabe* ("beef pot") or *agura-nabe* ("cross-legged pot"), from the custom of sitting cross-legged on the floor while the ingredients simmered. Later it was given and retained the name *sukiyaki*.

The term *sukiyaki* actually appears earlier, in an Edo cookbook entitled *Shirōto bōchō* ("Cooking for Amateurs"). As may be seen in Plate 178, the earlier dish consisted merely of fish slices grilled on a type of plow (*suki*). The sukiyaki that became so popular in the Meiji period, however, consists of beef slices and vegetables simmered in broth, a dish well suited to the Japanese palate, and is now a part of Japanese cuisine.

In 1871–73, a number of Western-style restaurants

177. *Biidoroshi* ("Glass-Blowers"), from the print series *Fujin shokunin burui* ("Types of Female Craftsmen"), by Utamaro.

178. *Sukiyaki*, from *Shirōto bōchō* ("Cooking for Amateurs").

151

opened and flourished along with the beef houses. As part of the general Westernization of eating habits, bread was baked, but then did not succeed as a staple food. The most popular form of bread was *anpan*, a sweet bun filled with *an* (sweet azuki bean paste).

Throughout the Meiji period (1868–1912), everyday fare for most people continued to be traditional in style and content, largely unchanged from Edo times. As Western dishes gained increasing acceptance, however, they were often altered to suit Japanese taste, creating in time a new culinary climate. Westernization affected eating utensils as well: dining tables, coffee cups, spoons, forks, salt shakers, sugar bowls, and the like became increasingly common.

In the Taishō era (1912–26), the influence of Western cuisine extended even to home cooking. Consumption of meat, butter, Worcestershire sauce, and other Western foods rose conspicuously. At the same time, two new dishes became popular: *tonkatsu*, an adaptation of pork cutlet, and "curry rice," based on Indian-style curry. The latter was especially quick to catch on, becoming a favorite light meal seemingly overnight.

The use of individual serving tables and trays dropped steadily in the Taishō era; their place was taken by low folding tables called *chabudai*, around which the whole family could gather, seated on the floor. Western-style plates, glass tumblers, coffee cups, soup plates, forks, and knives became still more prevalent. Many people ate from Western dishes with chopsticks, however, and Taishō eating establishments began providing throwaway *waribashi* (half-split wooden chopsticks), a practice that continues to this day.

Increasing mechanization in the Meiji and Taishō periods affected the manufacture of porcelain and glass, making cheap, mass-produced wares available to all. Traditional lacquer ware, impossible to mass-produce, was priced out of competition and slowly faded from the market.

179. Food vessels used in the household of the potter Kenkichi Tomimoto (rice bowls, tea cups, plate).

Amid this increasing uniformity, Sōetsu Yanagi (1889–1961) emerged as a spokesman for the enduring value of handmade things, for the forgotten beauty of ordinary, everyday utensils. The influential *mingei* (folkcraft) movement that he promoted nourished a number of outstanding artists, including potters like Kenkichi Tomimoto (1886–1963; Pl. 179), Shōji Hamada (1894–1978), and Kanjirō Kawai (1899–1966).

Another man of great creativity and lasting influence was the potter Rosanjin Kitaōji (1883–1959). Dissatisfied with the manufactured dishes available, he began to make his own. His works perfectly matched the foods served in them in line with his belief that "serving vessels are the clothing of food." His style derived in large part from Oribe wares of the Momoyama period, and from Shino, Kenzan, and Seto wares. A great epicure and restaurateur, Rosanjin was also a great artist who re-created the beauty of traditional Japanese utensils in modern times.

THE PLATES

page 1. "March," detail of eight-fold screen, *Tsukinami fū-zoku* ("Seasonal Customs and Monthly Amusements"). Late Muromachi period. Tokyo National Museum.

pages 2–3. Green bamboo rafts
Raft at left
FOOD: (from left) grilled rock trout (*aburame*); garnish: *sansho* sprigs (*kinome*); fern fiddleheads; whitebait fried in egg yolk; garnish: pickled plum (*umeboshi*)
ARRANGEMENT: three-variety scattered style

Raft in center
FOOD: (from left) lily bulbs with sea urchin; *iwatake*; shrimp, tiny bamboo shoots, rape blossoms; octopus eggs; garnish: *sansho* sprigs (*kinome*)
ARRANGEMENT: original

Raft at right
FOOD: tilefish sushi wrapped in cherry leaves; ginger stalks
ARRANGEMENT: rice-bale style

pages 4–5. Same dishes as on pages 6–7.

pages 6–7. Spring (left) and autumn (right) arrangements.
Spring
Bowl, Kutani porcelain, overglaze enamels. D. 32.5 cm. Early Edo period.
FOOD: Boiled bamboo shoots; garnish: *sansho* sprigs (*kinome*)
ARRANGEMENT: piled-up style

Saké cup, Negoro lacquer, H. 5.5 cm. Momoyama period.

Autumn
Gourd-shaped saké bottle, Imari porcelain, paulownia and maple pattern, cobalt underglaze. H. 20.5 cm. Edo period.

Hexagonal saké cup, monochrome Oribe ware. H. 6.4 cm. Momoyama period.

Saké cup, sea bream design, overglaze enamels, by Aoki Mokubei. D. 8.4 cm. Late Edo period.

Square plate, Bizen ware style, by Rosanjin Kitaōji. 27.0 × 26.2 cm.
FOOD: grilled mackerel stuffed with shiitake mushrooms; garnish: fern leaf (inedible)
ARRANGEMENT: piled-up style

page 8. Detail of six-fold screen, *Maple Viewing at Takao* by Kanō Hideyori. Late Muromachi period. Tokyo National Museum.

1 (page 17). New Year
Cut-cornered tray (*sumikiri oshiki*), Negoro lacquer. W. 38.7 cm. Early Muromachi period.

Bowl, Negoro lacquer. D. 14.3 cm. Early Muromachi period.
FOOD: Kyoto–Osaka area style *ozōni* (New Year soup) with grilled *mochi*

Mukōzuke, section of green bamboo stalk.
FOOD: dried persimmon and grated daikon radish

2 (pages 18–19). Spring
Left page (from top)
Saké cups, Negoro lacquer. D. 10.3 cm. Momoyama period.
Stand (*haidai*) for saké cups, Negoro lacquer. D. 15.7 cm. Muromachi period.

Tiered food boxes, red and black lacquer. Contemporary.
FOOD: (clockwise from right) Rice: "scattered" sushi (*chirashi-zushi*) topped with egg threads; garnish: *sansho* sprigs (*kinome*)
Mukōzuke: sea bream sashimi stuffed with dry fermented beans (*Daitoku-ji nattō*); rape blossoms
Simmered course (*takimono*): shrimp, fern fiddleheads, soybean milk skin (*yuba*); garnish: *sansho* sprigs (*kinome*)

Saké cup, porcelain and overglaze enamels, by Fujio Koyama. D. 8.8 cm.

Right page
Cherry blossom-shaped saké server (*kannabe*) by Kanchi. L. 16.5 cm. Edo period.

Abalone-shaped *mukōzuke* dish, Oribe ware. L. 16.0 cm. Momoyama period.
FOOD: mixed shellfish sashimi
ARRANGEMENT: jumbled style

Lidded bowl, red and black lacquer, bamboo and wisteria pattern. D. 13.0 cm. Momoyama period.
FOOD: clear soup; wheat gluten ball filled with quail meat and decorated with thread spool pattern; chrysanthemum leaves; garnishes: *Suizenji nori*, *yuzu* citron peel
ARRANGEMENT: bowl style

3 (page 20). Spring
Peony-shaped *mukōzuke* dishes, peony design, overglaze enamels, by Ogata Kenzan. W. 16.6 cm. Middle Edo period.
FOOD: (from top) sea bream sashimi (with skin); garnishes: *Kamogawa nori*, slivered ginger, *wasabi* horseradish
ARRANGEMENT: piled-up style

FOOD: fava beans and tiny bamboo shoots
ARRANGEMENT: jumbled style

FOOD: shrimp; garnishes: *shiso* flowers (*hojiso*), *bakudai*
ARRANGEMENT: piled-up style

4 (page 21). Spring
Gourd-shaped saké bottle, Imari porcelain, paulownia and chrysanthemum design, cobalt underglaze. H. 17.2 cm. Edo period.

Rectangular bowl, Gray Shino ware, "frame" style with grass design. L. 21.9 cm. Momoyama period.
FOOD: grilled rock trout (*aburame*); garnish; *sansho* sprigs (*kinome*)

Three dishes, Kutani porcelain, pomegranate design, overglaze enamels. D. 13.6 cm. Early Edo period.

5 (page 22). Summer
Green bamboo basket.
FOOD: sea bream sushi wrapped in bamboo grass leaves
ARRANGEMENT: piled-up style

Teabowl, porcelain, net pattern, cobalt underglaze. D. 11.0 cm. Late Ming dynasty.
FOOD: water shield (*junsai*)

6 (page 23). Summer
Deep bowl, porcelain, spatter pattern and calligraphy, cobalt underglaze, by Rosanjin Kitaōji. D. 25.0 cm.
FOOD: steamed abalone; garnish: *shiso* flowers (*hojiso*)
ARRANGEMENT: piled-up style

Saké cup, striped rim, by Fujio Koyama.
Saké cup, celadon, by Fujio Koyama.

Lidded bowl, *maki-e* lacquer, wave design. D. 13.7 cm. Meiji period.
FOOD: thick clear soup with sea eel and okra; garnish: pickled plum (*umeboshi*)
ARRANGEMENT: bowl style

7 (page 24). Summer
High-footed large bowl, Imari porcelain, cobalt underglaze. D. 31.0 cm. Edo period.
FOOD: deep-fried sea bream (*akōdai*); garnish: hydrangea leaves
ARRANGEMENT: original

Rectangular *mukōzuke* dishes, Oribe ware style, by Rosanjin Kitaōji. L. 20.6 cm.

8 (page 25). Summer
Octagonal saké glasses by Junshirō Satō. H. 4.9 cm.

Handled bowl, porcelain, Buddhist disciple (*arhat*) design, cobalt underglaze. L. 22.9 cm. Late Ming dynasty.
FOOD: grilled sea eel
ARRANGEMENT: piled-up style

9 (page 26). Autumn
Large saké cup, Karatsu ware. H. 4.6 cm. Momoyama period.
FOOD: salted sea cucumber (*konowata*)

Square plate, Kutani porcelain, tortoiseshell pattern, overglaze enamels. W. 19.5 cm. Edo period.
FOOD: Saké-grilled tilefish
ARRANGEMENT: piled-up style

10 (page 27). Autumn
Saké bottle, Gray Shino ware, stripe pattern. H. 19.0 cm. Momoyama period.

Hexagonal saké cup. D. 6.7 cm. Momoyama period.

Two *mukōzuke* dishes, autumn grasses pattern, by Ogata Kenzan. D. 14.3 cm. Middle Edo period.
FOOD: (top) raw tuna and mountain yam
ARRANGEMENT: original

FOOD: (bottom) grilled *matsutake* mushroom and *mizuna* greens
ARRANGEMENT: jumbled style

11 (page 28). Autumn
Saké bottle, Seto ware. H. 15.0 cm. Momoyama period.

Deep bowl, Kutani porcelain, bird-in-pine design, overglaze enamels. D. 20.6 cm. Early Edo period.
FOOD: deep-fried shrimp balls; taro stalks; okra; garnishes: *yuzu* citron zest slivers, black sesame seeds
ARRANGEMENT: three-variety nestled style

Hexagonal saké cup, Kiseto ware. D. 6.9 cm. Momoyama period.

Lidded bowl, black on red lacquer, autumn grasses design. D. 13.9 cm. Late Edo period.
FOOD: thick clear broth; steamed grated turnip stuffed with tilefish; garnish: *wasabi* horseradish
ARRANGEMENT: bowl style

12 (page 29). Autumn
Tea cup, "wheat-straw" pattern, by Rosanjin Kitaōji. H. 7.7 cm.

Square bowl, Monochrome Oribe ware, incised and openwork patterns. W. 16.5 cm. Momoyama period.
FOOD: mackerel and tilefish sushi
ARRANGEMENT: rice-bale style

13 (page 30). Winter
Pouring bowl, Tamba ware. L. 22.2 cm. Early Edo period.
FOOD: grilled taro (*ebi-imo*)
ARRANGEMENT: piled-up style

Three small dishes, snowy pines design, by Ogata Kenzan. D. 13.0 cm. Middle Edo period.

14 (page 31). Winter
Lacquerer's workboard. 42.4 × 27.7 cm. Modern.
FOOD: assortment of deep-fried foods: oyster mushrooms, ginkgo nuts, waterchestnuts (cut to resemble pine cones), lily bulbs, wheat gluten, sliced chestnuts, soybean milk skin (*yuba*); garnish: dried magnolia leaf and pine needles
ARRANGEMENT: original

Saké bottle, figures and calligraphy, by the nun Rengetsu. H. 12.0 cm. Meiji period.
Saké cup, birds and poem, by the nun Rengetsu. D. 6.8 cm. Meiji period.

15 (page 32). Winter
Saké bottle, Seto ware, tea whisk design, overglaze enamels. H. 14.8 cm. Late Edo period.
Saké cup, Shino ware style, plum blossom design, by Rosanjin Kitaōji. D. 5.5 cm.

Square dish, December, from a set of twelve, mandarin ducks and plum blossom design, by Ogata Kenzan. W. 16.8 cm.

Middle Edo period.
FOOD: shrimp, sea urchin, and trefoil stems
ARRANGEMENT: jumbled style

16. Three sashimi arrangements (from top)
Rectangular dish, Imari porcelain, bamboo design, cobalt underglaze. L. 19.8 cm. Late Edo period.
FOOD: sea bream; garnishes: fern fiddleheads, *wasabi* horseradish
ARRANGEMENT: flat style

Plate, Imari porcelain, Shinto banner design, overglaze enamels. D. 16.5 cm. Late Edo period.
FOOD: sea bream; garnishes: *wasabi* horseradish, *iwatake*, rape blossoms
ARRANGEMENT: piled-up style

Rectangular dish, Imari porcelain, cobalt underglaze and iron glaze. L. 14.5 cm. Late Edo period.
FOOD: sea bream; garnishes: *wasabi* horseradish, *iwatake*
ARRANGEMENT: cedar-tree style

17. Serving dish arrangements (from top)
Plate by Shōji Hamada. D. 27.0 cm.
FOOD (*takiawase*): simmered shrimp; soybean milk skin (*yuba*); rape blossoms
ARRANGEMENT: three-ingredient nestled style

Plate, Mashiko ware, stripe pattern.
FOOD: omelette rolls stuffed with eel
ARRANGEMENT: rice-bale style

Bowl, Bizen ware style, incised stripe pattern, by Rosanjin Kitaōji. D. 16.0 cm.
FOOD (pickles): *takuan* daikon pickle; turnip leaves and stalks
ARRANGEMENT: three-ingredient nestled style

18–20. Identical ingredients and arrangements (five-variety scattered style) using three different vessels.
Vessels (from top): Black lacquer square. W. 30.5 cm. Contemporary.
Round tray, red and black lacquer. D. 24.0 cm. Contemporary.
Dansk plate. D. 25.5 cm.
FOOD: (left) deep-fried baby sea bream; deep-fried *tara* tree shoots
(center) shrimp; *udo* (*Aralia cordata*) wrapped in soybean milk skin (*yuba*)
(right) parboiled *yomena* leaves and field horsetail (*tsukushi*) dressed with sesame paste

21. Waiting room for the tea ceremony (*yoritsuki*)
SCROLL: Plum tree and calligraphy by Ikkyū Sōjun. Ink on paper. Muromachi period.

Noodle-sauce cups, Imari porcelain, bamboo grass design, cobalt underglaze. H. 6.0 cm. Edo period.
Tray, pine wood, poem and calligraphy by the nun Rengetsu. D. 38.5 cm. Meiji period.
POEM: Changing into kindness
    the cruelty of one who would not give
    me shelter for the night—
    A single spray of blossoms
    under the hazy moon.

22. *Oshiki* tray, black lacquer.

Mukōzuke dish, Shino ware, wave and plover design. W. 15.7 cm. Momoyama period.
ARRANGEMENT: piled-up style

FOOD: sea bream sashimi, day lily (*kanzō*) stems, *iwatake*

Four nested bowls, black lacquer, Rikyū style.
FOOD: rice; miso soup with *ebi-imo* yam cut in tortoiseshell (hexagonal) pattern, azuki beans, and mustard

Rikyū-bashi chopsticks

23. Stand (*haidai*), *maki-e* on black lacquer, New Year's design, by Sano Chōkan. H. 12.6 cm. Late Edo period.
Saké cups, Negoro lacquer. D. 10.3 cm. Momoyama period.

Saké server (*kannabe*), floral lozenge and grass pattern (and cloisonné lid), by Kojōmi. 19.0 × 13.0 cm. Edo period.

Lidded bowl, *maki-e* lacquer, camellia design. D. 12.3 cm. Edo period.
ARRANGEMENT: bowl style
FOOD: thick clear soup with shrimp, *yuzu* citron, carrot, lettuce hearts, and oyster mushrooms

24. Covered rice container, round tray, and rice paddle, black lacquer.

Square dish, Oribe ware, pine tree design. L. 20.0 cm. Momoyama period.
ARRANGEMENT: piled-up style
FOOD: grilled pompano
Green bamboo serving chopsticks

25. Chinese bellflower-shaped bowl, Kakiemon style porcelain, overglaze enamel. D. 18.2 cm. Edo period.
ARRANGEMENT: jumbled style
FOOD: vinegared crab, *suizenji nori*; garnish: *bōfū*

Bowl, Kiseto ware style, by Rosanjin Kitaōji. D. 20.4 cm.
ARRANGEMENT: two-ingredient nestled style
FOOD (*takimono*): simmered turnips, shrimp, *yuzu* citron zest slivers
Green bamboo serving chopsticks

Saké bottle, Bizen ware. H. 11.3 cm. Momoyama period.
Hexagonal saké cup. D. 7.7 cm. Momoyama period.

26. Small covered lacquer bowl with flared lip, by Sōtetsu I. D. 6.1 cm. Edo period.
FOOD: thin, clear stock with pickled plum (*umeboshi*) and butterbur (*fuki*) bud

Saké server (*kannabe*), floral lozenge and grass pattern (and Oribe ware lid), by Kojōmi. 19.0 × 13.0 cm. Edo period.

Hassun tray, cedar wood.
ARRANGEMENT: scattered style
FOOD: tiny green pickled daikon radish (arranged in rice-bale style); mullet roe (arranged in piled-up style)
Green bamboo serving chopsticks

27. Hot water ewer, dipper, and rectangular tray, black lacquer.
FOOD: hot water and *yunoko* scorched rice

Small bowl, Iga ware. H. 8.5 cm. Momoyama period.
ARRANGEMENT: three-ingredient nestled style
FOOD: pickled sliced turnip stems rolled in thin pickled turnip slices, turnip greens, *takuan* daikon pickles
Green bamboo serving chopsticks

28. Box (*fuchidaka*), black lacquer. W. 16.8 cm. Meiji period.
FOOD: sweet bean paste (soft) confection (called *matsugasane*)

Tray, green lacquer, gold scroll pattern, by Ōko. D. 21.5 cm.

Momoyama period.
ARRANGEMENT: three-variety scattered style
FOOD: "dried" (hard) confections—plum blossom, pine needle, and *noshi* banner shapes

TEABOWL: Okugōrai type (a type of Karatsu ware). Momoyama period.

29. Modern lidded bowls, lacquer (clockwise from back left)
a. Gold-leaf decoration, lion, peony, and scrolling vine design. D. 13.3 cm.
b. Black lacquer, fine concentric ridges. D. 13.9 cm.
c. Brown and red lacquer, gold leaf, reed and heron design. D. 13.3 cm.
d. Clear (outside) and black (inside) lacquer. D. 14.4 cm.
e. Black and red lacquer, gold leaf, heron and autumn grasses design.
f. Black lacquer, gold and silver leaf, sun and moon pattern, by Rosanjin Kitaōji. D. 12.7 cm.
g. Red and black lacquer, color reversed on lid and body, autumn grasses pattern. D. 13.8 cm.
h. Black lacquer with gold *maki-e*. D. 14.2 cm.
i. Translucent brown (outside) and black (inside) lacquer. D. 12.8 cm.
j. Black, red, and yellow lacquer, paulownia design. D. 13.3 cm.
k. Red on black lacquer, brushstroke pattern. D. 14.2 cm.
l. Red lacquer, chosen by the tea master Katagiri Sekishū. D. 14.3 cm.

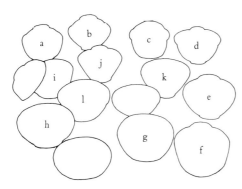

30. Two nested bowls, lacquer and gold leaf, peach design. Largest D. 14.0 cm. Momoyama period. Suntory Museum of Art.

31. Two nested bowls, lacquer and gold leaf. Largest D. 13.0 cm. Momoyama period. Suntory Museum of Art.

32. Bowl and cover, Yoshino lacquer. D. 13.2 cm. Edo period. Suntory Museum of Art.

33. Three nested bowls, lacquer and gold leaf, paulownia design. Largest D. 14.2 cm. Edo period. Suntory Museum of Art.

34. Three nested bowls, lacquer and gold leaf, paulownia, bamboo grass, and phoenix designs. Largest D. 14.2 cm. Edo period. Suntory Museum of Art.

35. Covered bowl, Hidehira lacquer. D. 12.2 cm. Momoyama period. Suntory Museum of Art.

36. Five nested bowls, *maki-e* lacquer, paulownia design. Largest D. 13.8 cm. Momoyama period. Suntory Museum of Art.

37. Set of three covered bowls, Meigetsu type, lacquer with shell inlay, cherry blossom pattern. D. 14.1 cm. Momoyama period. Meigetsu-in temple, Kamakura.

38. Bowls, red and black lacquer. Rice bowl D. 12.4 cm. Momoyama period.

39. Rectangular teabowl, Black Oribe ware, flower design. D. 12.4 cm. Momoyama period.

40. Teabowl, Incised Karatsu ware. D. 12.3 cm. Momoyama period.

41. Teabowls (clockwise from top left)
Shino ware. D. 13.0 cm. Momoyama period.
Red Raku ware by Hisada Sōzen. Edo period.
Shallow teabowl, Oribe ware. Momoyama period.
Irregular, squat teabowl, Black Oribe ware. Momoyama period.
Incised *mishima* teabowl. Yi dynasty.

42. Cylindrical tea cup, Mino ware, geometric pattern. H. 10.0 cm. Early Edo period. Japan Folkcraft Museum, Tokyo.

43. Tea cup by Kanjirō Kawai. Iron oxide underglaze. Ōhara Museum of Art, Kurashiki.

44. Three tea cups by Shōji Hamada. H. 9.3 cm.

45. Rice bowl, Seto ware, dot pattern. D. 12.8 cm. Early Edo period. Japan Folkcraft Museum, Tokyo.

46. Rice bowl, Imari porcelain, fan design, cobalt underglaze. D. 11.8 cm. Edo period. Japan Folkcraft Museum, Tokyo.

47. Rice bowl, Seto porcelain, willow tree design, cobalt underglaze. D. 12.4 cm. Edo period. Japan Folkcraft Museum, Tokyo.

48. Rice bowl, Seto ware, net pattern, iron underglaze. D. 12.0 cm. Edo period. Japan Folkcraft Museum, Tokyo.

49. Rice bowl, Seto ware, "wheat-straw" pattern. D. 12.5 cm. Edo period. Japan Folkcraft Museum, Tokyo.

50. Modern dishes and plates (clockwise from top left)
Long, footed plate, Oribe ware style, by Rosanjin Kitaōji. 48.7 × 25.2 cm.
Cross-shaped dish, Oribe ware style, by Rosanjin Kitaōji. 20.4 × 19.6 cm.
Three plates, leaf design, by Rosanjin Kitaōji. D. 19.2 cm.
Irregular plate by Rosanjin Kitaōji. 22.6 × 21.0 cm.
Leaf-shaped plate, Oribe ware style, by Rosanjin Kitaōji. 20.5 × 9.5 cm.
Dish for serving eel by Shōji Hamada. 24.2 × 13.3 cm.
Dish for serving eel by Shōji Hamada. 25.0 × 13.7 cm.
(center) Plate, cross pattern, by Rosanjin Kitaōji. D. 17.0 cm.

51. Large dish, Karatsu ware, pine tree design. D. 35.8 cm. Momoyama period. Idemitsu Museum of Arts.

52. Large dish, Karatsu ware, iris design. D. 28.7 cm. Momoyama period.

53. Large dish, Kutani porcelain, lotus pond and kingfisher

design. D. 36.3 cm. Early Edo period. Japan Folkcraft Museum, Tokyo.

54. Square dish, Kutani porcelain, rice field paths design. 23.3 × 20.3 cm. Early Edo period.

55. Platter, Imari porcelain, depicting map of Japan and Pacific region. D. 52.4 cm. Late Edo period. Saga Prefectural Museum.

56. Platter, Imari porcelain, roundels depicting the Fifty-Three Stages of the Tōkaidō Highway (from Nihonbashi on the right-hand corner to Sanjō Ōhashi in the center). D. 64.5 cm. Late Edo period.

57. Dish, Imari porcelain, resist rabbit design, sprayed cobalt underglaze. D. 19.3 cm. Edo period. Imaemon Antique Ceramics Center.

58. Dish, Kakiemon style porcelain, sleeve design. D. 18.7 cm. Edo period.

59. Dish, Nabeshima porcelain, cord and tassle design. D. 20.2 cm. Edo period. Suntory Museum of Art.

60. Plate, Nabeshima porcelain, jar design. D. 15.4 cm. Edo period.

61. Plate, Nabeshima porcelain, scattered book design. D. 21.2 cm. Edo period.

62. Plate, Imari porcelain, camellia design. D. 20.3 cm. Edo period. Japan Folkcraft Museum, Tokyo.

63. Plate, Imari porcelain, geometric pattern. D. 11.8 cm. Edo period. Japan Folkcraft Museum, Tokyo.

64. Plate, Seto ware, "horse-eye" pattern, iron underglaze. Late Edo period. Japan Folkcraft Museum, Tokyo.

65. Plate, Seto ware, iris design. D. 36.3 cm. Edo period. Japan Folkcraft Museum, Tokyo.

66. Plate, Seto ware, landscape design. D. 36.0 cm. Edo period. Japan Folkcraft Museum, Tokyo.

67. Four square dishes (from a set of twelve) by Ogata Kenzan. (clockwise from upper right)
February: pheasant and cherry blossoms
March: skylark and wisteria
December: poems (calligraphy)
June: wild pinks and cormorant
W. 16.6–16.9 cm. Middle Edo period.

68. Square dish by Ogata Kenzan; Mt. Fuji design painted by his brother, Ogata Kōrin. 22.0 × 21.8 cm. Middle Edo period. Suntory Museum of Art.

69. Modern serving bowls (left, top to bottom)
Shallow bowl by Shōji Hamada. D. 25.5 cm.
Shallow bowl by Kanjirō Kawai. D. 21.6 cm.
Shallow bowl, bamboo grass design, by Shōji Hamada. D. 25.7 cm.
(right) Large bowl, camellia design, by Rosanjin Kitaōji. D. 43.0 cm. H. 22.2 cm.

Fan-shaped bowl, Oribe ware style, by Rosanjin Kitaōji. 21.0 × 23.6 cm.

70. Large bowl, Kiseto ware, radish design. D. 24.8 cm. Momoyama period.

71. Large bowl, Karatsu ware, flower and grass design. D. 34.3 cm. Momoyama period. Suntory Museum of Art.
Deep bowl, Karatsu ware, flower and grass design. D. 16.0 cm. H. 11.2 cm. Momoyama period. Suntory Museum of Art.

72. Shino and Oribe pieces (clockwise from top right)
Square bowl, Shino ware, autumn grass design. 29.5 × 9.9 cm. Momoyama period. Suntory Museum of Art.
Shallow bowl, Gray Shino ware, willow and bird design. D. 24.9 cm. Momoyama period. Suntory Museum of Art.
Lidded box, Oribe ware, bridge design. 18.0 × 20.0 cm. Momoyama period. Suntory Museum of Art.
Handled bowl, Oribe ware, "sand billow" shape, flower design. 28.1 × 25.0 cm. Momoyama period. Suntory Museum of Art.

73. Shallow bowl, Green Kutani porcelain, *noshi* banner design, overglaze enamels. Edo period.

74. (top piece; underside) Large shallow bowls, Green Kutani porcelain, flower and vine pattern, overglaze enamels. D. 42.8 cm. Edo period. Suntory Museum of Art.
Large shallow bowls, Green Kutani porcelain, floating fan design, overglaze enamels. D. 34.6 cm. Edo period.

75. Small bowl, Imari porcelain, bellflower pattern. D. 12.7 cm. Edo period. Japan Folkcraft Museum, Tokyo.

76. Small foliate bowl, Imari porcelain, chrysanthemum pattern. D. 13.7 cm. Edo period. Japan Folkcraft Museum, Tokyo.

77. Large shallow bowl, Imari porcelain, landscape design, cobalt underglaze. D. 47.7 cm. Early Edo period. Japan Folkcraft Museum, Tokyo.

78. Modern *mukōzuke* dishes (top row, from left)
Square dish, bamboo design, by Kanjirō Kawai. 9.0 × 8.7 cm.
Square dish by Kanjirō Kawai. 7.8 × 7.6 cm.
Cylindrical piece by Kanjirō Kawai. D. 10.7 cm.
Octagonal piece, Oribe ware style, by Rosanjin Kitaōji. D. 8.5 cm. H. 9.5 cm.
Octagonal piece, bamboo design, cobalt underglaze, by Rosanjin Kitaōji. D. 8.0 cm. H. 9.3 cm.

(middle row, from left)
Oval dish, Hagi ware. 12.3 × 10.8 cm.
Trifoliate piece in the style of Ninsei, by Kyūhō. D. 8.1 cm. H. 8.3 cm.
Red Shino ware style, "wheat-straw" pattern, by Rosanjin Kitaōji. D. 9.6 cm. H. 9.0 cm.

(bottom row, from left)
Spouted dish, Karatsu ware style.
Tulip-shaped piece, Kiseto ware style, by Rosanjin Kitaōji. D. 9.0 cm. H. 8.8 cm.
"Split pod"-shaped piece by Rosanjin Kitaōji. D. 11.0 cm. H. 8.7 cm.

79. Hexagonal deep *mukōzuke* dish, Oribe ware. D. 7.5 cm. H. 11.0 cm. Momoyama period.

80. Hexagonal deep *mukōzuke* dish, Oribe ware. D. 5.0 cm. H. 8.0 cm. Momoyama period.

81. Footed deep *mukōzuke* dish, Oribe ware. 6.0 × 6.0 cm. Momoyama period. Suntory Museum of Art.

82. Fan-shaped *mukōzuke* dish, Oribe ware. Hyōgo Prefecture Ceramic Museum.

83. Crescent-shaped *mukōzuke* dish, Oribe ware. L. 15.8 cm. Early Edo period.

84. Rhomboid *mukōzuke* dish, Oribe ware. L. 20.3 cm. Early Edo period.

85. Plover-shaped *mukōzuke* dish, Oribe ware, wisteria design. W. 15.8 cm. Momoyama period.

86. Depressed-rim *mukōzuke* dish, Oribe ware. W. 14.5 cm. Momoyama period.

87. Boat-shaped *mukōzuke* dish, Oribe ware, flower and dart design. L. 17.0 cm. Momoyama period.

88. "Sand billow"-shaped *mukōzuke* dish, Oribe ware, flower design. Momoyama period.

89. Foliate *mukōzuke* dish, monochrome Oribe ware, mule and rider design. D. 16.2 cm. Momoyama period.

90. Foliate *mukōzuke* dish, monochrome Oribe ware, heron design. D. 16.0 cm. Momoyama period. Suntory Museum of Art.

91. *Mukōzuke* dishes, Kiseto ware, flower and grass designs. D. 14.5–15.5 cm. Momoyama period. Hatakeyama Collection.

92. Cylindrical *mukōzuke* dish, Shino ware, willow design. H. 9.7 cm. Momoyama period.

93. Persimmon flower-shaped *mukōzuke* dishes, Karatsu ware. L. 10.0 cm. Early Edo period.

94. Camellia-shaped *mukōzuke* dishes, camellia pattern, by Ogata Kenzan. D. 10.5 cm. Middle Edo period. Nezu Institute of Fine Arts.

95. *Mukōzuke* dishes, Karatsu ware style, flower and *dango* (skewered rice balls) design, by Ogata Kenzan. L. 15.5 cm. Middle Edo period.

96. Set of *mukōzuke* dishes, maple leaves in the Tatsuta River design, by Ogata Kenzan. D. 18.2 cm. Middle Edo period. Itsuō Art Museum, Ikeda, Osaka.

97. Lacquered picnic box set (with pewter saké bottles), *maki-e* lacquer, scenes from the Yoshiwara pleasure quarter. H. 32.3 cm. Middle Edo period. Suntory Museum of Art.

98. Tiered food box, *maki-e* lacquer, *noshi* banner design. H. 21.4 cm. Edo period. Japan Folkcraft Museum, Tokyo.

99. Tiered food box, *maki-e* lacquer, umbrella design. Edo period.

100. Ewer, Negoro lacquer. D. 35.0 cm. H. 36.0 cm. Muromachi period. Suntory Museum of Art.

101. Hot water ewer, lacquer. D. 27.2 cm. Edo period. Japan Folkcraft Museum, Tokyo.

102. Saké server, Negoro lacquer, L. 23.0 cm. H. 12.2 cm. Muromachi period.

103. Saké server, Shino-Oribe ware. H. 16.8 cm. Early Edo period.

104. Gourd-shaped saké server, Kakiemon style porcelain, grapevine, bird, and cord design. 18.5 × 13.0 × 16.0 cm. Edo period. Suntory Museum of Art.

105. Saké server, Nagasaki glass. D. 20.5 cm. H. 17.0 cm. Edo period. Suntory Museum of Art.

106. Geometric saké server, Satsuma ware. H. 16.0 cm. Late Edo period.

107. Contemporary teapots and cups
(clockwise from top right)
Teapot, Onta ware. H. 12.8 cm.
Teapot, Shussai ware. H. 12.6 cm.
Tea cup by Jirō Kinjō (Okinawa).
Three Oribe and Shino style tea cups.
Tea cup, Mashiko ware.

108. Modern saké bottles and cups
(far left, front to back)
a. Saké cup, Bizen ware, by Tōyō Kanashige. H. 4.4 cm.
b. Saké cup, Hagi ware, by Kyūsetsu Miwa. H. 5.5 cm.
c. Saké cup, Bizen ware, by Yū Fujiwara. H. 6.0 cm.
(on tray, clockwise from back left)
d. Saké cup, hatch and dot pattern.
e–h. Saké bottles: two on ends by Rosanjin Kitaōji.
e. Bizen ware style. H. 12.1 cm.
h. Shino ware style. H. 11.2 cm.
f, g. Two bottles in center by Shōji Hamada. H. 13.3 and 12.5 cm.
i. Saké cup, Red Shino ware style, grass design, by Rosanjin Kitaōji. H. 4.0 cm.
j. Saké cup, Hagi ware, by Shimbei Sakakura XIV. H. 4.3 cm.
k. Saké cup, Korean style engobe, by Masaya Yoshimura. H. 3.6 cm.
l. Footed saké cup, porcelain. H. 5.3 cm.
Plum blossom-shaped tray, red lacquer, by Tōru Matsuzaki.

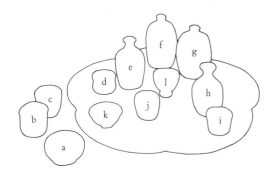

109. Saké bottle for use on a boat, Tamba ware, red slip engobe and natural ash glaze. H. 27.9 cm. Middle Edo period. Japan Folkcraft Museum, Tokyo.

110. Candle-shaped saké bottle, Tamba ware, tube-trailed pattern. H. 15.7 cm. Late Edo period. Japan Folkcraft Museum, Tokyo.

111. Saké bottle, Bizen ware, natural ash glaze. H. 18.2 cm. Momoyama period.

112. Purse-shaped saké bottle, Tamba ware. H. 18.6 cm. Edo period. Tamba Pottery Museum, Sasayama.

113. Saké bottle, Imari porcelain, pine design (reverse, bamboo design), cobalt underglaze. H. 23.0 cm. Edo period. Suntory Museum of Art.

114. Gourd-shaped saké bottle, Shino-Oribe ware, grapevine design. H. 27.9 cm. Momoyama period.

115. Twisted gourd-shaped saké bottle, Kutani porcelain, flower and grass design, overglaze enamels. H. 20.1 cm. Edo period. Tokyo National Museum.

116. Twisted gourd-shaped saké bottle, Imari porcelain. H. 20.5 cm. Edo period. Suntory Museum of Art.

117. Sauce server, spring grasses design, by Ogata Kenzan. 6.7 × 9.8 cm. Middle Edo period. Suntory Museum of Art.

118. Sauce servers by Rosanjin Kitaōji. H. 9.5 cm. Kitamura Art Museum, Kyoto.

119. *Takatsuki* type tray-table, Negoro lacquer. H. 32.5 cm. W. 37.2 cm. Muromachi period (dated 1416). Isonokami Shrine, Tenri, Nara.

120. *Tsuigasane* type tray-table, Negoro lacquer. H. 12.4 cm. W. 39.7 cm. Muromachi period (soon after 1567).

121. *Kakeban* type tray-table, Negoro lacquer. H. 28.0 cm. W. 27.5 cm. Kamakura period.

122. Butterfly-leg type tray-table and two bowls from seven nested bowls, *maki-e* lacquer, paulownia design. Table: 36.5 × 36.0 × 9.0 cm. Bowl: D. 14.0 cm. Momoyama period. Suntory Museum of Art.

123. Tray, polychrome lacquer. D. 26.5 cm. Japan Folkcraft Museum, Tokyo.

124. Box table, green and red lacquer. H. 20.5 cm. W. 32.0 cm. Edo period.

125. Noodle-sauce cups, Imari porcelain, cobalt underglaze. Edo period.

126. Chopstick rests, vegetable shapes.
Rikyū-bashi chopsticks, chopstick rest by Rosanjin Kitaōji.

127. "April," detail of eight-fold screen, *Tsukinami fūzoku* ("Seasonal Customs and Monthly Amusements"). Late Muromachi period. Tokyo National Museum.

128. Pot with pointed bottom, earthenware. Middle Jōmon period. Waseda University.

129. Spouted pot, earthenware. H. 12.7 cm. Late Jōmon period.

Ōme Municipal Museum of Provincial History, Tokyo.

130. Small bowl, earthenware. H. 7.6 cm. Yayoi period. Meiji University.

131. Large jar, earthenware. H. 35.3 cm. Yayoi period. Meiji University.

132. Canteen-shaped flask (*teibei*), Sué ware. H. 20.2 cm. Late Tumulus period. Takasaki City Educational Committee.

133. Barrel-shaped flask (*yokobei*), Sué ware. H. 20.5 cm. Middle Tumulus period. Osaka City Educational Committee.

134. Bowl, three-colored glaze. D. 26.9 cm. Nara period. Shōsō-in.

135. Carafe, clear glass. H. 27.2 cm. Nara period. Shōsō-in.

136. Foliate dish, lacquer on wood. 39.0 × 37.0 cm. Nara period. Shōsō-in.

137. Courtier's meal on round, pedestalled tray-table. *Ruijūzōyō-shō* ("Compendium of Miscellaneous Affairs"; detail). Edo period copy. Suntory Museum of Art.

138. Court meal, *Ruijūzōyō-shō* ("Compendium of Miscellaneous Affairs"; detail). Edo period copy. Suntory Museum of Art.

139. Meal for the guest of honor, *Ruijūzōyō-shō* ("Compendium of Miscellaneous Affairs"; detail). Edo period copy. Suntory Museum of Art.

140. *Tonjiki* (midday snack); *Ruijūzōyō-shō* ("Compendium of Miscellaneous Affairs"; detail). Edo period copy. Suntory Museum of Art.

141. Urn, *maki-e* lacquer, bamboo, paulownia, and phoenix design. Heian period. Tamukeyama Shrine, Nara.

142. Dishes, ash glaze. Heian period.

143. Bowls, plates, and ewer, green glaze. Ewer H. 24.4 cm. Late Heian period. Gumma Prefectural Museum.

144. *Bandainagon ekotoba* scroll (detail). Late Heian period. Idemitsu Museum of Arts.

145. *Gakizōshi emaki* ("Scrolls of Hungry Demons"; detail). Latter half 12th century. Tokyo National Museum.

146. *Yamai no sōshi* ("Diseases Scroll"; detail). Latter half 12th century.

147. *Gosannen gassen emaki* scroll ("The Three Years' War"; detail). 1347. Tokyo National Museum.

148. *Kasuga gongen kenki emaki* scroll ("Miracles of the Shinto Deities of Kasuga"; detail). 1309. Imperial Household Collection.

149. *Boki ekotoba* scroll ("The Life of Priest Kakunyo"; detail). 1351. Nishi-Hongan-ji temple, Kyoto.

150. Jar, Old Seto ware, stamped pattern of plum blossoms,

iron underglaze. H. 29.0 cm. Kamakura period. Suntory Museum of Art.

151. Bucket-shaped serving dish, Negoro lacquer. D. 32.8 cm. 1307.

152, 153. *Shuhanron ekotoba* scroll ("Debate over Food and Wine"; details). Muromachi period.

154. Rice container, Negoro lacquer. D. 27.8 cm. Muromachi period.

155. Hexagonal bowl with legs, Negoro lacquer. D. 38.0 cm. Muromachi period. Suntory Museum of Art.

156. From *Shokunin zukushi-e* ("Catalogue of Craftsmen")—The Bentwood (*magemono*) Craftsmen. Edo period copy. Suntory Museum of Art.

157. *Rakuchū Rakugai* ("Sights In and Around the Capital"; detail of six-fold screen). Momoyama period.

158. *Namban* ("Southern Barbarian"; detail of six-fold screen). Momoyama period. Suntory Museum of Art.

159. Hexagonal tiered food box, gold lacquer with shell inlay. H. 10.5 cm. Momoyama period. Suntory Museum of Art.

160. Spice container set (small porcelain jars covered with *maki-e* lacquer with floral motifs). D. 22 cm. Momoyama period. Kōdai-ji temple, Kyoto.

161. Teabowl, black Raku ware, by Chōjirō. D. 13.5 cm. Momoyama period.

162. *Kawaguchi yūkaku-zu* ("The Kawaguchi Pleasure District" screen; detail of ten-fold screen). Edo period.

163. Banquet scene, from *Shiroto bōchō* ("Cooking for Amateurs"), book by Asano Kōzō, pub. 1803. National Diet Library.

164. Sushi making, from *Shiroto bōchō* ("Cooking for Amateurs"), book by Asano Kōzō, pub. 1803. National Diet Library.

165. *Kaiseki* setting, from *Ryōri haya shinan*, book in 4 vols. by Daigo Sanjin, pub. 1822. Tokyo Kasei Gakuin College.

166. Chinese-style vegetarian meal, from *Fucha ryōri shō* ("A Selection of Vegetarian Food"), book by Mitatsu Nishimura, pub. 1772. National Diet Library.

167. *Yaozen* restaurant, from *Edo kōmei kaitei zukushi* ("Famous Restaurants of Edo"), print series by Andō Hiroshige. Suntory Museum of Art.

168. *Aoyagi* restaurant, from *Edo kōmei kaitei zukushi* ("Famous Restaurants of Edo"), print series by Andō Hiroshige. Suntory Museum of Art.

169. Boat-shaped bowl, Kakiemon style porcelain, overglaze enamels. L. 26.5 cm. Edo period. Suntory Museum of Art.

170. Saké bottle, Imari porcelain, iron glaze and overglaze enamels. H. 22.4 cm. Edo period.

171. Lidded bowl, Imari porcelain, overglaze enamels, flower carts, and women design. 32.0 × 29.9 cm. Edo period. Suntory Museum of Art.

172. Teabowl, scale pattern, overglaze enamels, by Nonomura Ninsei. D. 12.4 cm. Edo period. Kitamura Museum of Art.

173. Tea (*sencha*) set by Aoki Mokubei. Edo period. Tokyo National Museum.

174. Tray with cut-corners, porcelain, flowers, birds, and fish design, overglaze enamels, by Okuda Eisen. W. 30.5 cm. Edo period. Tokyo National Museum.

175. Large bowl, cherry blossoms and maple leaves design, overglaze enamels, by Nin'ami Dōhachi. D. 39.0 cm. Edo period. Suntory Museum of Art.

176. Advertising circular from Kagaya. Edo period.

177. *Biidoroshi* ("Glass-Blowers"), from *Fujin shokunin burui* ("Types of Female Craftsmen"), print series by Kitagawa Utamaro. Edo period. Kōbe City Museum.

178. *Sukiyaki*, from *Shiroto bōchō* ("Cooking for Amateurs"), book by Asano Kōzō, pub. 1803. National Diet Library.

179. Food vessels used in the household of the potter Kenkichi Tomimoto (rice bowls, tea cups, plate). Kenkichi Tomimoto Memorial Museum.

図 版 目 録

24. 黒真塗利休形飯器　丸盆　飯杓子
織部松文四方皿　桃山時代　（まながつお味噌漬　重ね盛り）

25. 柿右衛門色絵花鳥文桔梗形鉢　江戸時代（水前寺海苔、蟹酢の物、防風添え　混ぜ盛り）
魯山人作黄瀬戸鉢　（海老と蕪の煮合せ、針柚子　二種寄せ盛り）
備前火欅徳利　桃山時代
椿手六角ぐい呑　桃山時代

26. 初代宗哲作端反小吸物椀　江戸時代（ふきのとう、梅肉仕立て）
古浄味作花菱竹地紋四方入角燗鍋・織部蓋　江戸時代
八寸　（青味大根　俵盛り　からすみ　重ね盛り）

27. 黒真塗湯桶・湯の子掬い・長盆
伊賀沓鉢　桃山時代　（千枚漬、日野菜、たくあん　三種寄せ盛り）

28. 一閑片木目縁高　明治時代　（松襲ね　京都　松屋製）
往古作和独楽干菓子盆　桃山時代　（梅花、松葉、結び熨斗　亀屋伊織製）
奥高麗茶碗（唐津）　桃山時代

p.67—73. 食器挿絵　「茶之湯献立指南」「守貞漫稿」「料理早指南」「素人庖丁」「新撰庖丁梯」「和漢三才図会」より

29. 近代の椀
　a. 牡丹唐草文長寛写し箔絵椀
　b. 黒糸目椀
　c. 葦鷺文漆絵椀
　d. 外春慶塗中黒塗椀
　e. 鷺秋草文漆絵椀
　f. 魯山人作日月椀
　g. 色変り秋草漆絵椀
　h. 糸目蓋裏稲穂蒔絵椀
　i. 中黒外溜塗椀
　j. 桐漆絵椀
　k. 朱刷毛目椀
　l. 石州好み煮物椀（朱塗メハジキ）

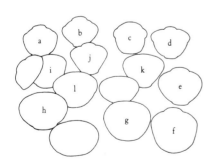

30. 桃枝漆絵椀　桃山時代　サントリー美術館

31. 箔押漆絵椀　桃山時代　サントリー美術館

32. 吉野椀　江戸時代　サントリー美術館

33, 34. 桐竹鳳凰漆絵三ツ椀　桃山時代　サントリー美術館

35. 秀衡椀　桃山時代　サントリー美術館

36. 桐蒔絵五ツ重椀　桃山時代　サントリー美術館

37. 明月椀　桃山時代　明月院

38. 片身替四ツ椀　桃山時代

39. 黒織部四方茶碗　桃山時代

40. 彫唐津茶碗　桃山時代

41. 志野刷毛目茶碗　桃山時代
久田宗全作赤楽茶碗　江戸時代
赤織部幾何文平茶碗　桃山時代
黒織部沓茶碗　桃山時代
彫三島平茶碗　李朝

42. 美濃幾何文筒湯呑　江戸初期　日本民藝館

43. 河井寛次郎作　白釉呉須鉄絵茶碗　大原美術館

44. 浜田庄司作湯呑

45. 瀬戸志野釉丸紋碗　江戸初期　日本民藝館

46. 伊万里染付団扇文碗　江戸時代　日本民藝館

47. 瀬戸呉須絵柳文飯茶碗　江戸時代　日本民藝館

48. 瀬戸灰釉網目文碗　江戸時代　日本民藝館

49. 瀬戸麦藁手碗　江戸時代　日本民藝館

50. （左上から時計回りに）織部組皿　織部クルス皿　木の葉文皿　伊賀鉋目角皿　織部木の葉皿（以上魯山人作）　筋文うなぎ用角皿　丸紋うなぎ用角皿（以上浜田庄司作）　クルス文丸皿（魯山人作）

51. 絵唐津松文大皿　桃山時代　出光美術館

52. 絵唐津菖蒲文大皿　桃山時代

53. 古九谷蓮池にかわせみ文色絵皿　江戸初期　日本民藝館

54. 古九谷色絵畦道文角皿　江戸初期

55. 伊万里染付世界地図文大皿　江戸後期　佐賀県立博物館

56. 伊万里染付東海道五十三次文大皿　江戸後期

57. 伊万里染付吹墨手兎図皿　江戸時代　今右衛門古陶磁参考館

58. 柿右衛門色絵誰が袖文中皿　江戸時代

59. 鍋島色絵房紐文七寸皿　江戸時代　サントリー美術館

60. 鍋島色絵三壺文皿　江戸時代

61. 鍋島色絵冊子散らし文皿　江戸時代

62. 伊万里熨斗椿文赤絵中皿　江戸時代　日本民藝館

63. 伊万里染付割筆文皿　江戸時代　日本民藝館

64. 瀬戸馬の目文皿　江戸時代　日本民藝館

65. 瀬戸菖蒲文石皿　江戸時代　日本民藝館

66. 瀬戸山水文石皿　江戸時代　日本民藝館

67. 乾山作十二ヵ月色紙皿　「二月」「三月」「十二月」「六月」　江戸中期

68. 乾山作雪景富士図角皿（光琳画）　江戸中期　サントリー美術館

69. （左上から）浜田庄司作丸紋平鉢　河井寛次郎作平鉢　浜田庄司作笹紋平鉢　魯山人作紅白椿文鉢　魯山人作扇形鉢

70. 黄瀬戸大根文鉦鉢　桃山時代

71. 唐津草花文平鉢　唐津菖蒲文鉢　桃山時代　サントリー美術館

72. （右上から）志野薄文四方鉢　鼠志野柳文平鉢　織部蓋物　織部花文洲浜形手鉢　桃山時代　サントリー美術館

73. 青手古九谷熨斗文平鉢　江戸初期

74. 青手古九谷松樹文平鉢（裏）　江戸初期　サントリー美術館
青手古九谷扇面流平鉢　江戸初期

75. 伊万里染付桔梗文小鉢　江戸時代　日本民藝館

76. 伊万里染付菊文小鉢　江戸時代　日本民藝館

77. 伊万里染付山水文大鉢　江戸初期　日本民藝館

78. 近代の向付
（上列左から）河井寛次郎作四方笹文向付　四方色替り向付　筒向付　魯山人作　織部八角向付　染付竹文八角向付
（中列左から）萩沓形向付　久宝作仁清風輪花向付　魯山人作麦藁手紅志野向付
（下列左から）絵唐津写し片口　魯山人作黄瀬戸チューリップ形向付　魯山人作唐津割山椒向付

79. 織部筒向付　桃山時代

80. 織部草絵六角筒向付　桃山時代

81. 織部高脚四方入隅向付　桃山時代　サントリー美術館

82. 織部格子に瓢文扇面向付　桃山時代　兵庫県陶藝館

83. 織部三日月形向付　江戸初期

84. 織部菱形絵替り向付　江戸初期

85. 織部千鳥形向付　桃山時代

86. 織部切落とし向付　桃山時代

87. 織部舟形向付　桃山時代

88. 織部洲浜形向付　桃山時代

89. 総織部騎馬人物文平向付　桃山時代

90. 総織部鷺文平向付　桃山時代　サントリー美術館

91. 黄瀬戸草花文絵替平向付　桃山時代　畠山記念館

92. 絵志野柳萩絵筒形向付　桃山時代

93. 絵唐津柿の花向付　江戸初期

94. 乾山作椿意匠向付　江戸中期　根津美術館

95. 乾山作唐津風花団子文向付　江戸中期

96. 乾山作龍田川向付　江戸中期　逸翁美術館

97. 吉原風俗蒔絵提重　江戸中期　サントリー美術館

98. 蒔絵熨斗文重箱　江戸時代　日本民藝館

99. 蒔絵金銀梨地傘文重箱　江戸時代

100. 根来湯桶　室町時代　サントリー美術館

101. 漆塗湯桶　江戸時代　日本民藝館

102. 根来銚子　室町時代

103. 志野織部銚子　江戸初期

104. 柿右衛門様式葡萄文酒注　江戸時代　サントリー美術館

105. 長崎ガラス藍色酒注　江戸時代　サントリー美術館

106. 薩摩黒釉六角酒注　江戸後期

107. 現代の土瓶と湯呑
（右上から時計回りに）小鹿田焼無地土瓶　出西焼土瓶　金城次郎作湯呑（沖縄）　加藤重高作総織部湯呑　志野湯呑二口　益子焼湯呑

108. 近代の徳利と石盃
　　a. 金重陶陽作備前ぐい呑
　　b. 三輪休雪作萩ぐい呑
　　c. 藤原雄作備前ぐい呑
　　d. 赤絵金丸文ぐい呑
　　e. 魯山人作備前徳利
　　f, g. 浜田庄司作徳利二口
　　h. 魯山人作志野徳利
　　i. 魯山人作紅志野風草文ぐい呑
　　j. 十四代坂倉新兵衛作萩焼ぐい呑
　　k. 吉村昌也作盃（笠間焼）
　　l. 脚付盃
松崎融作梅花形漆膳

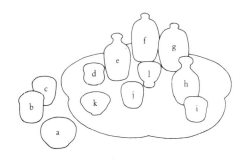

109. 丹波船徳利　江戸中期　日本民藝館

110. 丹波筒流文ろうそく徳利　江戸後期　日本民藝館

111. 備前火襷無徳利　桃山時代

112. 丹波蔦口巾着形徳利　江戸後期　丹波古陶館

113. 伊万里染付松竹文徳利　江戸時代　サントリー美術館

114. 志野織部瓢形徳利　桃山時代

115. 古九谷色絵草花文捻瓢形徳利　江戸時代　東京国立博物館

116. 伊万里瑠璃釉捻瓢形徳利　江戸時代　サントリー美術館

117. 乾山作春草文汁注　江戸中期　サントリー美術館

118. 魯山人作醤油注二口　近代　北村美術館

119. 根来高坏　室町時代（応永23年銘）　石上神宮

120. 根来衝重　室町時代

121. 根来懸盤　鎌倉時代

122. 桐蒔絵蝶足膳　桐蒔絵椀（七ツ重椀のうち二口）　桃山時代　サントリー美術館

123. 塗分盆　日本民藝館

124. 外縁漆内朱塗箱膳　江戸時代

125. 伊万里染付ソバ猪口　江戸時代

126. 野菜形箸置　利休箸　魯山人作「流枕」文扇面箸置

127. 月次風俗図屏風・「四月」　室町末　東京国立博物館

128. 甕形土器　縄文中期　早稲田大学

129. 注口土器　縄文後期　青梅市郷土博物館

130. 小型鉢形土器　弥生時代　明治大学

131. 壺形土器　弥生時代　明治大学

132. 提瓶　須恵器　古墳後期　高崎市教育委員会

133. 横瓶　須恵器　古墳中期　大阪府教育委員会

134. 奈良三彩鉢　奈良時代　正倉院

135. 白瑠璃瓶　奈良時代　正倉院

136. 漆彩絵花形皿　奈良時代　正倉院

137—140. 「類聚雑要抄」（江戸後期模本・部分）　サントリー美術館

137. 丸形高坏に盛られた貴族食

138. 公卿用食膳

139. 尊者用食膳

140. 屯食（とんじき）

141. 桐竹鳳凰蒔絵瓶子　平安時代　手向山神社

142. 灰釉耳皿　平安時代

143. 緑釉陶器（水注、碗、皿）　平安後期　群馬県立博物館

144. 伴大納言絵詞（部分）　12世紀後半　出光美術館

145. 餓鬼草紙（部分）　12世紀後半　東京国立博物館

146. 病草紙（部分）　12世紀後半

147. 後三年合戦絵巻（部分）　1347年　東京国立博物館

148. 春日権現験記絵巻（部分）　1309年　宮内庁

149. 慕帰絵詞（部分）　1351年　西本願寺

150. 古瀬戸飴釉印花梅花文瓶子　鎌倉時代　サントリー美術館

151. 根来菜桶　1307年

152、153. 酒飯論絵詞（部分）　室町時代

154. 根来飯器　室町時代

155. 根来六角足付鉢　室町時代　サントリー美術館

156. 職人尽絵のうち曲げもの師　（江戸時代模本）　サントリー美術館

157. 洛中洛外図屏風（部分）　桃山時代

158. 南蛮屏風（部分）　桃山時代　サントリー美術館

159. 縞蒔絵六角三ツ重食籠　桃山時代　サントリー美術館

160. 薬味壺（陶胎）　桃山時代　高台寺

161. 長次郎作黒楽茶碗　桃山時代

162. 川口遊廓図屏風（部分）　江戸時代

163. 本膳料理の饗応〔「素人庖丁」享和三年（1803）刊より〕

164. すし作り（「素人庖丁」）

165. 会席の図　〔「料理早指南」文政五年（1822）刊より〕

166. 精進の卓袱料理〔「普茶料理抄」西村未達著　明和9年（1772）刊より〕

167. 広重　「江戸高名会亭尽・八百善」　サントリー美術館

168. 広重　「江戸高名会亭尽・青柳」　サントリー美術館

169. 伊万里色絵舟形鉢　江戸時代　サントリー美術館

170. 伊万里斜線文角瓶　江戸時代

171. 伊万里色絵美人花車図蓋物　江戸時代　サントリー美術館

172. 野々村仁清作色絵鱗波文茶碗　江戸時代　北村美術館

173. 青木木米作煎茶セット　江戸時代　東京国立博物館

174. 奥田頴川作呉須赤絵花鳥魚文隅切膳　江戸時代　東京国立博物館

175. 仁阿弥道八作雲錦手大鉢　江戸時代　サントリー美術館

176. 加賀屋の引札　江戸時代

177. 歌麿　「婦人職人分類」より「びいどろ師」　江戸時代　神戸市立博物館

178. 鋤焼の図　（「素人庖丁」より）

179. 富本家常用食器　近代　富本憲吉記念館

INDEX

ACKNOWLEDGMENT

The author and publishers wish to express their gratitude to Messrs. Keizō Saji, Sōshirō Yabumoto, and to Mrs. Michiko Beppu of the Chikuyō-tei restaurant, without whose assistance, energy, and inspiration this volume would not have been possible, and to the many museums, temples, shrines, and private collectors whose permission has allowed the reproduction here of these many vessels, picture scrolls, and screens of the finest quality.

Sidney B. Cardozo

Hasshōkan

Hanayo Hori

Ryō Hosomi

Tanekichi Isozaki

Miyo Kaizuka

Hirokazu Kojima

Ryōji Kuroda

Hiroaki Man'no

Tarōemon Nakazato

Michiyasu Narita

Fujiko Okina

Gengo Shiozawa

Toshikazu Sugita

Takako Takaya

Yōko Tanaka

Takashi Yanagi

BOOK DESIGN
Shigeo Katakura

定価6,900円
in Japan